More Praise for *F*

"Roman Catholic apologists often ~~~~~ ~~~~~ ~~~~~ ~~~~~ churchs antiquity but seldom mention modern Roman Catholic theology, which often sounds as modern as liberal Protestantism. Karl Rahner, one of the most influential Roman Catholic theologians of the twentieth century, whose prominence was evident at the Second Vatican Council, is one of the best examples of Roman Catholicism's modernity. Camden Bucey's fair-minded and careful assessment of Rahner's theology is valuable in itself, but doubly so for anyone wanting an introduction to modern Roman Catholicism's own contribution to liberal Christian theology."

—**D. G. Hart**, Distinguished Associate Professor of History, Hillsdale College

"For those interested in getting to the heart of Karl Rahner's theology of Trinitarian personality, Camden Bucey's treatment is exceptional. Bucey lauds Rahner's insistence that humanity receive the grace of God through communion with him, but the author exposes how Rahner's methodology—particularly his identifying of Christ's hypostatic union as conduit of ontological self-communication—falls short. Following in the path of Reformed biblical theologians Geerhardus Vos and Meredith Kline, Bucey shows how God gives himself to his people in a mystical and covenantal bond that has been brought about through the death and resurrection of Jesus Christ in history."

—**Danny Olinger**, General Secretary for the Committee on Christian Education, Orthodox Presbyterian Church; author, *Geerhardus Vos: Reformed Biblical Theologian, Confessional Presbyterian*

"Continuing in the confessional Presbyterian tradition of Geerhardus Vos, Cornelius Van Til, and Robert Strimple, Dr. Bucey not only clearly expounds and trenchantly critiques

Rahner's theological proposal, but also points the way forward to a consistently biblical and covenantal Trinitarian alternative."
   —**Lane G. Tipton**, Charles Krahe Chair of Systematic Theology and Associate Professor of Systematic Theology, Westminster Theological Seminary

"Karl Rahner was singularly important to modern theology—both as a key catalyst in the revival of interest in Trinitarian theology and as an important influence on Vatican II and the shaping of modern Catholicism—and yet his work is conceptually daunting for those unfamiliar with the concerns of the transcendental Thomism, which he helped to formulate, and has therefore remained something of a closed book to many Protestants. This volume by Camden Bucey offers both an accessible introduction to Rahner's thought and a critique from an avowedly Van Tillian perspective. Readers may not agree with all of Bucey's arguments and conclusions, but he nonetheless provides a dialogue point for engaging an important strand of modern Catholic thought and Van Tillian critiques of Catholic theology."
   —**Carl R. Trueman**, Professor of Biblical & Religious Studies, Grove City College

"Though Karl Rahner is among the most significant Roman Catholic theologians of the twentieth century, he is little known (and seldom read) by evangelical and Reformed theologians. Camden Bucey's fine study offers an excellent summary of Rahner's Trinitarian theology that promises to redress this problem. He not only provides a helpful explanation of Rahner's well-known Trinitarian axiom ('the "economic" Trinity is the "immanent" Trinity'), but also locates it within the broader context of Rahner's anthropocentric theology. While Bucey critically engages Rahner's theology from a Reformed perspective, he does so throughout in a careful, irenic, and constructive fashion."
   —**Cornelis P. Venema**, President and Professor of Doctrinal Studies, Mid-America Reformed Seminary

Karl

RAHNER

GREAT THINKERS

A Series

Series Editor
Nathan D. Shannon

Karl
RAHNER

Camden M. Bucey

P&R
PUBLISHING
P.O. BOX 817 • PHILLIPSBURG • NEW JERSEY 08865-0817

ISBN: 978-1-62995-165-2 (pbk)
ISBN: 978-1-62995-166-9 (ePub)
ISBN: 978-1-62995-167-6 (Mobi)

Printed in the United States of America

Library of Congress Cataloging-in-Publication Data

Names: Bucey, Camden M., author.
Title: Karl Rahner / Camden M. Bucey.
Description: Phillipsburg : P&R Publishing, 2019. | Series: Great thinkers | Includes bibliographical references and index.
Identifiers: LCCN 2019019040 | ISBN 9781629951652 (pbk.) | ISBN 9781629951669 (epub) | ISBN 9781629951676 (mobi)
Subjects: LCSH: Rahner, Karl, 1904-1984.
Classification: LCC BX4705.R287 B83 2019 | DDC 230/.2092--dc23
LC record available at https://lccn.loc.gov/2019019040

For Erica

CONTENTS

SERIES INTRODUCTION

Amid the rise and fall of nations and civilizations, the influence of a few great minds has been profound. Some of these remain relatively obscure, even as their thought shapes our world; others have become household names. As we engage our cultural and social contexts as ambassadors and witnesses for Christ, we must identify and test against the Word those thinkers who have so singularly formed the present age.

The Great Thinkers series is designed to meet the need for critically assessing the seminal thoughts of these thinkers. Great Thinkers hosts a colorful roster of authors analyzing primary source material against a background of historical contextual issues, and providing rich theological assessment and response from a Reformed perspective.

Each author was invited to meet a threefold goal, so that each Great Thinkers volume is, first, *academically informed*. The brevity of Great Thinkers volumes sets a premium on each author's command of the subject matter and on the secondary discussions that have shaped each thinker's influence. Our authors identify the most influential features of their thinkers' work and address them with precision and insight. Second, the series maintains a high standard of *biblical and theological faithfulness*. Each volume stands on an epistemic commitment to "the whole counsel of God" (Acts 20:27), and is thereby equipped for fruitful critical engagement. Finally, Great Thinkers texts are *accessible*, not burdened with jargon or unnecessarily difficult vocabulary. The goal is to inform and equip the reader as effectively as possible through clear writing, relevant analysis, and incisive, constructive critique. My hope is that this series will distinguish itself by striking with biblical faithfulness and the riches of the Reformed tradition at the central nerves of culture, cultural history, and intellectual heritage.

Bryce Craig, president of P&R Publishing, deserves hearty thanks for his initiative and encouragement in setting the series in motion and seeing it through. Many thanks as well to P&R's director of academic development, John Hughes, who has assumed, with cool efficiency, nearly every role on the production side of each volume. The Rev. Mark Moser carried much of the burden in the initial design of the series, acquisitions, and editing of the first several volumes. And the expert participation of Amanda Martin, P&R's editorial director, was essential at every turn. I have long admired P&R Publishing's commitment, steadfast now for over eighty-five years, to publishing excellent books promoting biblical understanding and cultural awareness, especially in the area of Christian apologetics. Sincere thanks to P&R, to these fine brothers and sisters, and to several others not mentioned here for the opportunity to serve as editor of the Great Thinkers series.

Nathan D. Shannon
Seoul, Korea

FOREWORD

You know it when you see it—a responsible theologian.

It's not the letters following one's name. It's not the dusty old books piled on one's desk. Nor is it the flattering endorsement by someone who describes one as "astute," "attentive," or "prescient."

A responsible theologian exhibits faith that seeks understanding, guided by the illumination of the Spirit—a faith that demonstrates the interrelationship of all truth. Without allowing doctrine to sit in abstract isolation from the whole, the good theologian is called to set his ideas within the full body of Christian thought, examining their veracity against the ultimate source of authority, the inspired text of Scripture. Furthermore, theology must never be an entrepreneurial endeavor; rather, it is undertaken on the shoulders of the two-millennia-strong Christian community. Finally, the theologian always understands his calling as worship.

But even for such a theologian, there is danger. It's possible to cover all these bases and still miss the mark by doing theology in the wrong place—that is, by doing theology in a proverbial "echo chamber." Echo chambers are hollow enclosures whose structure allows sound to reverberate. The idea is to enclose sound so that it continues to resound without depletion or intrusion.

Does this sound familiar? All that can be heard is a single voice, one so dominant that all other sounds are mere distractions to be ignored. This is precisely where theologians face danger. When our faith seeks understanding in the same predictable and finite place (the same authors, journals, and conversation partners) without ever listening to outside voices, we unwittingly find ourselves in a doctrinal echo chamber—the kind of "bubble trouble" that impoverishes theological reflection.

This leads to a question that may lie between you and this volume. Why would you invest time in a book that explores the theology of Karl Rahner? Perhaps you are intrigued by Rahner's theory of "anonymous Christianity." Or maybe you have heard someone describe him as the most influential Catholic theologian of the twentieth century. Even so, between now and the grave you have only a finite amount of reading time, so why give your attention to this topic? Camden Bucey provides a clear answer:

> Rahner remains widely influential in Catholic theology and a perennial dialogue partner in mainline Protestant thought. But he has gone virtually unnoticed in the confessionally Reformed church. Reformed theologians will have fundamental differences with Rahner regarding nearly all theological *loci*. Nevertheless, Rahner asked many important theological questions that deserve confessionally Reformed attention. Too easily, critics dismiss those who are most different from themselves without doing the homework of truly understanding them. We would be better served by studying Rahner on his own terms. Only then can we understand his theological formulations and see their value for ecumenical dialogue—not for the purpose

of superficial rapprochement, but for sharpening our understanding of God's desire to bring his people into consummated union and communion with him.

Camden Bucey is a responsible theologian. He is not only devoted to the principles of the Reformation, but also committed to helping readers escape from familiar echo chambers. He offers the gift of popping our provincial bubbles in favor of a far deeper and broader version of Reformed catholicity. Of the various ways in which he accomplishes this, there are a couple for which we should be particularly grateful.

Bucey's treatment of Rahner helps us to appreciate the holistic integration of theological thought—how doctrinal elements coalesce into an organic and unified system. As he states, "I want the reader to understand Rahner's theology as an organism." For Rahner, the key idea is the self-communication of God to humanity, a Trinitarian economy that unfolds through redemptive history, culminating in the victory of Christ, and experienced by men and women who are conformed to the divine image. Such integration provides needed inspiration and insight, particularly at a time when theological systems tend to fall short of a Trinitarian vision or fail to maintain a consistently Godward focus. These lessons are valuable, even when one doesn't agree with all of Rahner's conclusions.

Another vital contribution of Rahner concerns the personal nature of salvation, the uncreated grace of the triune God that renews a soul. As Bucey describes Rahner's view, "God communicates nothing less than himself to human beings, who are created specifically to receive this gift of self; therefore, the very fabric of man's nature discloses the characteristics of the God who desires to give himself to them." Here again, the timely importance of Rahner's point can hardly be overstated. In a day of sterile individualism, when autonomous freedom and the protection of personal interests keep us sequestered from one another, the message of the personal God who reconciles us in Trinitarian love is precisely what our lonely hearts need.

In short, Bucey's work makes me think of the opera by Michael Nyman, *The Man Who Mistook His Wife for a Hat*, based on a book by the same title, which featured research from neurologist Oliver Sacks. It tells the story of a patient who suffered from severe amnesia, a condition called *visual agnosia*. The disorientation not only impoverished his memory, but also affected his outlook on every dimension of life, including his most intimate relationship. It's a message that also pertains to theologians.

Because our theology relates to all of life and informs our most intimate relationships, we need to find liberation from our misleading myopias in service of a clearer vision of the triune God, a Reformed catholicity that is rooted in redemptive grace and has Christ at the center. This is the gift that Camden Bucey offers readers in these pages.

Chris Castaldo, PhD
Senior Pastor, New Covenant Church
Naperville, Illinois

ACKNOWLEDGMENTS

Many people have contributed to the completion of this book, which began as a PhD dissertation at Westminster Theological Seminary. First, I want to acknowledge my advisor, Dr. Lane G. Tipton. Without his friendship, guidance, theological insights, and initial suggestion to study Karl Rahner, this study would not have been possible. I also benefitted greatly from Dr. John P. Galvin at The Catholic University of America, under whom I studied for a semester. His kindness and patience eased the burden of my weekly commute from Philadelphia to Washington, DC Several friends and colleagues also helped me in a variety of ways. Special thanks are in order to Dr. Jeffrey C. Waddington, who read this work and offered valuable suggestions, and to Dr. James J. Cassidy, who assisted even as he worked on his own dissertation. The congregations of Calvary OPC (Glenside, PA), Bethel OPC (Wheaton, IL), and Hope OPC (Grayslake, IL) encouraged and supported me throughout my studies. I also wish to thank my editor, Dr. Nathan D. Shannon, whose insight and suggestions were tremendous. His patience and encouragement were most welcome during the arduous process of "de-dissertationing" this work. The author is solely to blame for any shortcomings.

Lastly, I want to thank my family. My sons, Derek, Miles, and David, sacrificed time with their father as I researched and wrote. My parents, Mark and Pamela Bucey, have also been faithful encouragers to me. I thank them for teaching me in word and deed what it means to have a personal relationship with the triune God. Most of all, I want to thank my loving and excellent wife, Erica, who has been unwavering in her support. I dedicate this work to her.

1

INTRODUCTION
AND OVERVIEW

While John Paul II or Benedict XVI could challenge for the role, a compelling case can be made that Karl Rahner, SJ (1904–84), was the most influential Catholic theologian of the twentieth century. Rahner's theological influence is perhaps most evident in the theology of the Second Vatican Council. Vatican II was itself the most significant event in Catholicism in the twentieth century, and Rahner's fingerprints are all over its documents. He did not write them, but his influence was pervasive. Some have even called him "the Holy Ghost writer of Vatican II." Rahner's theology is representative of a significant portion of post-Vatican II Catholicism, which itself is representative of a modern inclusivist approach to world religions, missions, and social engagement. Studying Rahner is a convenient shortcut for grasping a wide-reaching program of theology. It is odd that while Rahner is so significant and well-known in Catholic circles (whether loved or hated), he has gone relatively unnoticed in the Reformed tradition. We have had our hands full with theologians like Karl

Barth. Whereas hundreds, if not thousands, of volumes have been written on Barth, surprisingly few have been written on Rahner by Reformed theologians. My goal is to increase awareness of and promote deeper engagement with Rahner's theology in this brief introduction.

Rahner probes the deepest questions of Scripture: Who is God? Why did God create man? What is the future of humanity? In seeking to answer these questions, Rahner introduced or developed several theological principles that have received widespread adoption in Catholicism as well as Protestantism. He is well known for his Trinitarian axiom that "the 'economic' Trinity is the 'immanent' Trinity and the 'immanent' Trinity is the 'economic' Trinity."[1] While Rahner readily admits that he was not the first to present this idea, he nevertheless became the face of it and used the idea to develop a bold theology. Rahner is also known for his theology of the "anonymous Christian," the doctrine that people may be saved by Jesus Christ without ever hearing the gospel or professing faith in Christ—without even knowing or having heard of Jesus and his claims. Far from being discreet developments, these major theological contributions are deeply related.

Rahner was born in Freiburg im Breisgau, Germany, and raised in a Catholic home. In 1922, he entered the Society of Jesus. As part of his Jesuit training, Rahner studied philosophy at Feldkirch, Austria, and Pullach, Germany, and then theology in Valkenburg, Holland. After he was ordained in 1932, Rahner's Jesuit superiors directed him toward doctoral studies in philosophy. But after an unfortunate disagreement with his advisor over his approach to the philosophy of Thomas Aquinas, Rahner moved to studying theology. In 1936, he received his doctorate in theology from the University of Innsbruck in

---

1. Karl Rahner, *The Trinity* (New York: Crossroad, 1997), 22.

Austria and embarked upon a storied academic and ecclesiastical life. He saw himself censored by the magisterium, only to become a theological expert (*peritus*) and one of the most influential figures at the Second Vatican Council. He held several teaching posts, lectured widely, and wrote until his death, just twenty-five days after his eightieth birthday.[2] Several decades after his death, Rahner's legacy is still taking shape, and while the luster of Rahnerian studies may have dulled after the turn of the century, his influence is still felt.

Many excellent introductions to Rahner's theology exist, and I do not intend to replicate them.[3] I seek to do something different, something that will lead to a deeper understanding of Rahner's theology *as a whole*. We could simply list a dozen or so talking points on Rahner's theology, but then the reader would only obtain a glossary-level understanding of his theology, merely matching terms to discreet definitions. I want the reader to understand these doctrines individually, but, more importantly, I want the reader to understand Rahner's theology as an organism. As we begin with Rahner's Trinitarian theology and move through each of the traditional departments of theology, we will learn how Rahner develops one basic idea from beginning to end. Rahner's entire theological program is concerned to explain how God communicates himself to humanity, whom he created specifically for this purpose of self-communication. If we understand one thing about Rahner, it must be this point. Everything

2. Harvey Egan has compiled a chronology to accompany his brief biography of Rahner. Much of this information has been taken from Harvey Egan, *Karl Rahner: Mystic of Everyday Life* (New York: Crossroad, 1998), 14–27. For an extensive biography of both Karl and Hugo Rahner, see Karl H. Neufeld, *Die Brüder Rahner: Eine Biographie* (Freiburg: Herder, 1994).

3. For example, William V. Dych, *Karl Rahner* (Collegeville MN: Liturgical Press, 1992); Egan, *Karl Rahner*; Karen Kilby, *Karl Rahner: A Brief Introduction* (New York: Crossroad, 2007); Herbert Vorgrimler, *Understanding Karl Rahner: An Introduction to His Life and Thought* (New York: Crossroad, 1986).

Rahner does theologically is about this basic idea. By tracing that thread, we will gain an understanding of his Trinitarian axiom and his doctrine of the "anonymous Christian" much deeper than we could have through the standard handbook format.

Outline and Summary of the Argument

If Rahner's fundamental concern is to explain how God communicates himself to humanity, it is prudent to begin our exploration with the doctrine of God in order to describe precisely who God is. Rahner wants to maintain Nicene orthodoxy in his doctrine of the Trinity, but he is wary of some of its language, especially the language of "person." For Rahner, the personal subjectivity that applies to finite creatures is based upon limitation and the experience of "otherness." God does not experience himself in this way. He is not a subject before another subject, and therefore the divine essence cannot exist as a "person" in this sense. But that does not rule out the language of "person" in all senses. In terms of one notion of personhood, involving self-consciousness and free agency, God is the absolute "person," who gives the gift of himself to humanity. This is the essence of religion at the heart of the deepest question of both divine and human existence.

Rahner identifies the Father with the divine essence, while the Son and Spirit are not immediately identified with the essence, but rather with the Father.[4] This ordering is true for Rahner according to both divine ontology and economy, that is, in terms of God's being in himself and his actions with regard to creation. Ontology and economy are closely linked for Rahner, because the divine self-communication that humanity experiences in

---

4. Karl Rahner, *Foundations of Christian Faith: An Introduction to the Idea of Christianity* (New York: Seabury, 1978), 118.

history has its foundation in an eternal self-communication of the Father. As I will explain in the next chapter, the Father is properly the "absolute person" of the Godhead, while the Son and Spirit are communicated expressions of that absolute person. The economic Trinity should be understood as a new, concrete expression of the immanent Trinity. That is to say, the experience of the Trinity in history is an expression of an eternal reality—the Father's eternal self-communication of Son and Spirit. I will seek to demonstrate that, for Rahner, the unity of the Godhead is more basic than the diversity. This ontological "imbalance" ultimately compromises Rahner's theology of divine self-communication.

Man, as spirit in the world, is the capable recipient of God's gift of self. He is like a divinely created radio that is capable of receiving God's frequency. For Rahner, man possesses a twofold nature (spiritual and historical), which corresponds to God's twofold self-communication (Son and Holy Spirit). This relationship between the divine giver and his intended recipient is thoroughly personal. It is characterized by thought, emotion, and freedom. God freely chooses whether to communicate himself, and human beings freely choose whether to accept that communication. Seeing that the acceptance of such a gift would have significant effects upon humanity, Rahner must ensure that the gift is both given and received. He does so through his doctrine of Christ. When the eternal Son of God assumed a human nature, he became the new humanity, actualizing and intensifying the relationship between God and man. In his person, he guarantees the divine free offer of grace and its human acceptance. This solidifies God's saving purpose.[5] God does in the person of Christ what he intends to do for all who open themselves

5. Karl Rahner, "Christology within an Evolutionary View of the World," in *Theological Investigations*, trans. Karl-H. Kruger, vol. 5 (Baltimore: Helicon, 1966), 183–84.

in freedom. When a person accepts this divine gift of self, he or she receives an ontological self-communication that results in a change of being.

Although the main features of Rahner's theology complement one another, internal inconsistencies render his program implausible. Consequently, Rahner cannot deliver what he initially promises. God is seeking to give the gift of himself, and that self is triune. But in Rahner's theology, the content of the gift is the Father, identified with the divine essence, whereas the Son and Spirit are not directly identified with the essence. The Father communicates himself as Son and Spirit, but since the Godhead knows no genuinely personal "other" within the Trinity, Rahner is unable to identify another equally ultimate "person" to receive that intra-Trinitarian self-communication. And therefore, since the Son and Spirit are fundamentally self-communications of the Father, Rahner directs his Trinitarian theology externally by connecting his conceptions of *hypostasis* and divine self-communication to humanity through his Christology.

In practice, Rahner employs an anthropocentric theological method that begins with human experience, because Rahner must go to humanity in order to complete his doctrine of the Trinity. Still, his error is deeper than a misdirected methodology. Rahner cannot "solve" his problems by adopting a new starting point. These are deep-seated and systemic issues that, in spite of their common cause and relation, force his overall theological program into internal inconsistency. Rahner's insistence that God desires to give the gift of himself is biblical, but his theological formulations prevent him from explaining exactly how God gives the gift of himself if he is essentially Trinitarian. Rahner's theology is Trinitarian in delivery only, because unity and diversity are not ontologically absolute. Trinitarian diversity (the persons of the Godhead) serves as the means by which the unity of God (identified particularly with the Father) is communicated.

In his theology, Rahner seeks answers to the most important questions of human existence. I am thankful that he compels us to consider more deeply the wonderful mystery of God's relationship to his people. Yet, as I hope to demonstrate, the doctrines he formulates prove to be inadequate. Leaning upon the theology of Cornelius Van Til, I will seek to offer biblically sustainable answers to these questions. In response to Rahner's ontological model of self-communication, which leads to a change of being in its recipients, we will consider a covenantal framework for understanding the beatific vision. We will come to learn how, through covenant, God is conforming his people to his image, replicating his glory analogously in his people through the resurrected Christ (cf. Gen. 1:26–27; Rom. 8:29; 2 Cor. 3:18). Only by sharing in his image can God's people truly experience consummated union and communion with the *triune* God.

2

TRINITARIAN PERSONHOOD

Rahner's doctrine of the Trinity is at the heart of his theology, because it makes possible a genuine, substantial communication from God to his creatures. This communication is described in terms of a gift that is willingly given and then freely received. Such a self-communication involves a relationship between two persons, which establishes personhood as a critical feature of Rahner's theology. For our purposes, we will define personhood as the requisite characteristics of a person. Personality is the set of characteristics that distinguishes one person from another. By receiving the Son and Spirit as modes of divine self-communication, humanity is brought into a relationship with the intra-Trinitarian relations themselves.

What Does It Mean to Be a Person?

Since the fourth century, orthodox Christians have universally affirmed that God is three persons in one essence. This basic statement places limits on the ground that orthodox theologians may tread. At the same time, such a minimal definition is open to a variety of interpretations, since it does not define "persons" or "essence" precisely or describe the way in which they relate. As a result, a wide variety of theologies fit under the broad banner of orthodoxy. Theologians today struggle with many of the same issues that occupied Athanasius and the Cappadocian Fathers centuries before. What is a person with reference to the Godhead? How do the persons relate to the unity of the Godhead? How do they relate to one another? The ecumenical creeds offer guidelines for answering these questions according to a so-called "creedal" definition of "person." For example, a person is a distinct substance in the divine essence. Throughout this study, we will use the historical term *hypostasis* (plural, *hypostases*) when referring to this creedal definition of persons.

There are other senses in which we can speak of persons, which often cause confusion. There are many philosophical conceptions of personhood that are often imported into the language of persons in the ecumenical creeds. These are not necessarily opposed to the theology of the creeds; however, the semantic range of the terms are not coterminous. Philosophically speaking, we may refer to personhood as a confluence of rationality, self-awareness, consciousness, and volition. God is indeed a person in this sense, since we may ascribe rationality, self-awareness, consciousness, and volition to him. Nonetheless, whatever we say about God's personhood cannot be understood univocally to apply to human personhood or interpersonal experience.[1] Rahner

---

1. Rahner recognized these two senses of speaking: "The statement that God is a person, that he is a personal God, is one of the fundamental Christian assertions about God. But it creates special difficulties for people today, and rightly so. When we say that God is a person, and this in a sense which as yet has nothing to do with the question about the so-called three persons in God, then the question about the personal character of God becomes a twofold question: we can ask whether God in his own self must be called a person; and we can ask whether he is a person only in relation to us, and whether in his own self he is hidden from us in his absolute and transcendent distance. Then we would have to say that he is a person, but that

expresses this challenge: "We shall not have touched the real difficulties which such an assertion about God as person creates for
people today until we have discussed explicitly the relationship
between God and man, the self-communication of God to man in
grace as the transcendental constitution of man."[2] Moreover, it is
not clear how these things pertain specifically to the Father, Son,
and Holy Spirit as "persons."

While Rahner acknowledges the distinction between the
creedal and the philosophical senses of "person" as they pertain
to God, he also distinguishes between personhood as it relates
to God and personhood as it relates to finite subjects. The distinguishing factor between the two is the source of subjectivity.
The personal subjectivity applicable to finite creatures is predicated on limitation and the experience of "otherness." In terms
of essence, God has no "other," but that is not to say he has no
relations. God has no equal, though as *absolute* person, he is the
transcendental ground for all personality in the world. God is
a person who nevertheless remains shrouded in mystery.[3] He
has meaningful interactions with human beings, but the scope
and nature of these interactions exceed the limits of human
experience and cognition. While divine and human personhood
cannot be understood univocally, the difference between them
does not preclude the possibility of a real and meaningful interpersonal exchange.

---

he does not by any means for this reason enter into that personal relationship to us
which we presuppose in our religious activity, in prayer, and in our turning to God
in faith, hope and love" (Karl Rahner, *Foundations of Christian Faith: An Introduction
to the Idea of Christianity* [New York: Seabury, 1978], 73). See also his related discussion in Karl Rahner, "Oneness and Threefoldness of God in Discussion with Islam,"
in *Theological Investigations*, trans. Edward Quinn, vol. 18 (New York: Crossroad,
1983), 110.

2. Rahner, *Foundations of Christian Faith*, 73.

3. Ibid., 74.

The Self-Communicating God

Traditionally, theologians have distinguished between the immanent Trinity and the economic Trinity. The former pertains to God in himself and to the *hypostases* in relation to each other, apart from any external considerations. The latter pertains to God's being as it relates to creation, in which the Father, Son, and Spirit assume particular roles in order to create and redeem. Rahner challenges this distinction.

Immanent and Economic Identity in "Rahner's Rule"

Rahner is most commonly known for his so-called Trinitarian "rule," which states that "the 'economic' Trinity is the 'immanent' Trinity and the 'immanent' Trinity is the 'economic' Trinity."[4] This axiom has to do with the nature of God's existence and whether that existence differs according to God's relations *ad extra*.[5] The basic belief of monotheism is that God is fundamentally one God. Rahner thought that if certain safeguards were not put in place, the doctrine of the Trinity could contradict this basic tenet of the Christian faith. In order to maintain monotheism, Rahner argued that theologians must identify the immanent Trinity with the economic Trinity. Otherwise, they posit two Gods by suggesting that the God who is known in history is not the God who has existed from all eternity. The immanent Trinity is the economic Trinity,

---

4. Karl Rahner, *The Trinity* (New York: Crossroad, 1997), 22. This rule is widely recognized as Rahner's formulation, but he admits he did not introduce the idea: "We are starting out from the proposition that the economic Trinity is the immanent Trinity and vice versa. I do not know exactly when and by whom this theological axiom was formulated for the first time. But it seems to be established in theology today or is at least a theologoumenon that cannot be *a priori* rejected as heterodox, but can safely be used in theological reflection" (Rahner, "Oneness and Threefoldness of God in Discussion with Islam," 114).

5. Rahner, *The Trinity*, 48.

because the God who works in history is the same transcendent, eternal God.

If the purpose of inquiring into the nature of the Trinity is fundamentally the question of God's identity (who he is), then the theologian who desires to know who God is must first understand how God has made himself known. For Rahner this is directly a matter of human experience and where the Son and Spirit factor into the discussion so significantly. The Son and Spirit are the principal modes by which the one God makes himself known, not as independent existents, but as concrete modes of divine self-communication. Rahner guards against tritheism, but neither is his view modalism. He presents the Son and Spirit as eternal communications of the divine essence, which also become historical communications of that essence to humanity. The Trinity, argues Rahner, is not a concept that competes with monotheism; it is its "radicalization."[6]

To distinguish between the immanent Trinity and the economic Trinity is to distinguish between one God that saves and another that lies in abstract solitude. Therefore, Rahner rejects the distinction altogether, out of fear that a distinction between two Godheads would result. He argues that there is not a Trinity from eternity in back of the one revealed in salvation history. The Trinity is Trinity as such in the act of self-communication.[7]

---

6. Rahner, "Oneness and Threefoldness of God in Discussion with Islam," 109.

7. Catherine Mowry LaCugna has correctly identified this feature of Rahner's theology: "Both the distinction and the identity between the economic and immanent Trinity are conceptual, not ontological. There is only one trinitarian self-communication, which has both eternal and temporal aspects. Rahner does not mean, as in a tautology, that eternal and temporal realms are strictly identical, only that no gap may be inserted (as in neo-scholasticism) between 'God' and 'God for us.' Missions and processions are the same reality under different aspects. The eternal begetting of the Son is the eternal ground of the sending of the Son in the Incarnation. Likewise with the Holy Spirit. What distinguishes Rahner's axiom from neo-scholasticism is that he derives the axiom not from *a priori* principles but from salvation history" ("Introduction," in Rahner, *The Trinity*.

With this identification, Rahner introduced a unique tension between the traditional understanding of the divine essence and the contingent economic roles—or missions—of the *hypostases*.

The Father as the Unoriginate *Hypostasis*

Rahner's method for protecting monotheism leads him to understand the Father's existence differently from that of the Son and Spirit. Rahner employs an Eastern-inspired concept of their ontological relationship. He identifies the Father particularly as God because he is the unoriginate *hypostasis*: "The older creeds, and Eastern theology, start with the one God who is, and insofar as he is the Father."[8] The Father possesses a certain primacy over the Son and Spirit. He continues: "The Church confesses one almighty God who appears to her as the active Lord of salvation history and as creator of all finite reality . . . and confesses him as the 'Father.' . . . 'I believe in the one God, the Father almighty.'"[9] Rahner's formulation borders on subordinationism, in the sense that the Father in particular is the one God. He is the *hypostasis* most basically identified with the divine essence, and therefore bears primacy over the Son and Spirit. Since the Son and Spirit exist as self-communications of the Father, Rahner must find a way to maintain that these are eternal self-communications of the Father that are ontologically independent of and prior to creation. Otherwise, he would present a form of modalism.

Forms of modalism prioritize the divine essence over the persons (*hypostases*). In his operations relative to creation, God works in different modes. Whereas the essence remains unchanged, the persons are accommodated expressions of that unchanging essence. Quite simply, God changes by accommodating to

8. Ibid., 58.
9. Ibid.

different scenarios. To make sense of this, we might consider the essence to be God immanent and abstract and the persons as economic and concrete expression of God's being. Rahner is not a modalist according to this definition. He does not advocate for an abstract divine essence, because the essence is always comprehended in light of *hypostases* that subsist in the essence. Nonetheless, God is unoriginated, and as soon as we bring into view the Son, one who is originate as the begotten self-communication, then the unoriginated God comes to be known specifically as Father and, by implication, not as Son or Spirit.[10] The Trinity is a later concept, because it depends on unity.[11] Rahner believes this is why the Trinity unfolds later in salvation history.[12] The Father is the unoriginated God, identified with the divine essence, who reveals himself as Trinity in salvation history.[13] Since the unity is prior to the Trinity, and the Father is identified particularly with the unity of the Godhead, the Father must in some sense be prior to the Son and Spirit.

The Son and Spirit as Divine Self-Communication

The Son and Spirit are the modes of divine self-communication. Rahner calls them related moments distinct from one another, but nonetheless moments of the one self-communication of

---

10. Ibid., 60.

11. "But the Trinity, as such, a 'three-ness' and thus conceived as unity, is a later notion, since it puts the 'three' together into a unity with respect precisely to that (namely, 'person') through which they are properly distinct" (ibid., 59).

12. "We must avoid the misunderstanding that the one who acts in the Old Testament, insofar as he is the concrete partner, is the triune God. 'Triune God' and 'Trinity' are legitimate but secondary concepts which, after the events, synthesize the concrete experience of salvation and revelation in a 'short formula'" (ibid.).

13. "Here God is the 'Father,' that is, the simply unoriginate God, who is always known as presupposed, who communicates *himself* precisely when and because his self-communication does not simply coincide with him in lifeless identity. In this self-communication he stays the one who is free, incomprehensible—in a word, unoriginate" (ibid., 84).

God.[14] The term "moment" could be understood in a temporal sense, but for Rahner this is not temporal, but conceptual. The Father, Son, and Spirit are distinguished by their respective personal properties, processions, or modes of subsistence. In the Eastern tradition, the Son derives essentially from the Father, who is unbegotten. Here, Rahner moves the Eastern idea of derivation from the realm of ontological procession into the realm of personal interaction. In his formulation, the Son and Spirit proceed from the Father as his communication. Again, Rahner does not evoke temporal priority, nor does he intend to reject consubstantiality among the members of the Godhead. Although Son and Spirit are ways by which the eternal God communicates himself, we should not conclude that the *hypostases* are themselves created.[15] God concretizes himself in salvation history in a mode of factuality, but this can never lead to absolutizing that mode (Son or Spirit) over against the Father as unoriginate *hypostasis*. For Rahner, absolutizing a mode of divine communication tends toward polytheism, and so the Son and Spirit should always be understood as divine self-communications, inseparable from the Father-essence who communicates.

This brings us back to where Rahner begins: his Trinitarian axiom. The immanent Trinity is the economic Trinity and vice versa. Trinity, transcendental experience, and salvation history are inseparable, and it is pointless to speculate about a divine unity behind the revealed Trinity precisely because the Trinity is God's way of being for us.[16] Reformed theologians may become uneasy with this manner of speaking, because it seems to make

14. Ibid., 84–85.

15. Rahner, "Oneness and Threefoldness of God in Discussion with Islam," 115.

16. Rahner calls the Trinity a "mystery of salvation" (Rahner, *The Trinity*, 21). Rahner also rejects the idea that *hypostasis* is a univocal concept in God, because he believes this would lead to blurring the distinctions necessary to maintain three persons. So, technically, we equivocate when we say that the Father, Son, and Spirit are hypostases, since each subsists in the essence in its own unique way. See ibid., 29.

the Trinity a consequence of God's will to create and then save. This is why Rahner begins with an Eastern notion of essential derivation. The essence is specifically "the Father's godhead,"[17] and the Son and Spirit receive their essence from him, the unoriginate *hypostasis*.[18]

Hypostases and Personality

Since Rahner's concept of human personality presupposes an experience of the "other," he must determine how personality applies to the *hypostases* of the Godhead. The big question before us, then, is How is God able to exist as Trinity *ad intra*, apart from any consideration of that which is not God? If God has no ontological "other" prior to creation, it seems to preclude the possibility that we could speak of the divine essence existing as such a person—at least before he creates. In order to speak of the divine essence as necessarily a "person" or having "personality," because he "communicates" to others, we must invoke a different sense of the term. To answer this question, Rahner begins with human transcendental experience.

Consciousness and Trinitarian Personhood

In the philosophical sense that Rahner uses, personhood involves self-awareness and consciousness of one's distinction from others. This raises a tension within Rahner's theology. Because of his doctrine of divine unity, in which the Father-essence communicates Son and Spirit, Rahner cannot ascribe this type of personality to God. He must determine a different

17. Ibid., 16.
18. Ibid., 17. This is a debate within the history of Christianity. Thomas Aquinas and others maintain that the Son and Spirit derive or receive their essence from the Father. Calvin held that the Son was *autotheos* or divine in himself. As eternally begotten, he receives his personality from the Father, but not his essence.

type of Trinitarian personhood to describe the diversity in the Godhead, and since he particularly identifies the Father with the divine essence above the Son and Spirit, he must also determine whether the same notion of personhood may apply to each *hypostasis*.

While the church speaks of three *hypostases* or "subsistences," and we call these three "persons," Rahner insists that the church has not attempted to offer a definition of either term outside the context of Trinitarian theology—something more in line with his philosophical concerns.[19] Hence, we are left to answer many questions regarding God's interpersonal relationship with humanity. What is the nature of the relationship? Is there a genuinely bilateral exchange? Is this relationship conscious to the human subject, or does it somehow exist in preconscious, unthematic experience? Is it analogous to human-human relationships? And how does this pertain to the Father's relationship to the Son and Spirit? And perhaps most significantly, is the Father-human relationship somehow determinative of the Trinity itself? Rahner sees the immanent Trinity and the economic Trinity somewhat as two perspectives on the same reality. Evangelical and Reformed theologians understand the immanent Trinity as God's relationship to himself, whereas the economic Trinity has to do with God's relation to creation and specifically to humanity. From the vantage point of the immanent Trinity, the *hypostases* are "three relative concrete ways" the one and same God exists.[20] From the vantage point of the economic Trinity, the *hypostases* are "three concrete ways of being given."[21] They are concrete as opposed to abstract or conceptual, and are also really experienced in personal exchanges. They are relative as diverse modes of communication. The Son and Spirit are each given by the Father, yet the Son is not

19. Ibid., 73.
20. Ibid., 73–74.
21. Ibid.

the Spirit, nor is the Spirit the Son. This complies with his axiom that the immanent Trinity is the economic Trinity and vice versa. These are not distinct realities, but different perspectives on the same ontological reality of divine self-communication.

We come to know the eternal self-communication through the givenness of the Son and Spirit in salvation history.[22] This moment in time is not the beginning of the Son and Spirit; they are eternal. Nonetheless, they become known as given only when they are experienced and received concretely. This is a personal, communicative exchange, but it is economic. The eternal immanent givenness of the Son and Spirit is not a "personal" (again, in his philosophical sense) exchange between a diversity of hypostatic subjectivities, because, for Rahner, whatever we can say about human persons does not necessarily apply to God as he exists in himself:

> There exists in God only *one* power, *one* will, only one self-presence, a unique activity, a unique beatitude, and so forth. Hence, self-awareness is not a moment which distinguishes the divine "persons" one from another, even though each divine "person," as concrete, possesses a self-consciousness. Whatever would mean three "subjectivities" must be carefully kept away from the concept of person in the present context.[23]

Although he readily admits that the persons are conscious of themselves and of their distinctions from the other two persons, Rahner rejects the idea of three subjectivities or three consciousnesses in God. For example, "This distinctness is conscious. However, it is not conscious for three subjectivities, but it is the

---

22. This would certainly differentiate his formulation of "givenness" from a Reformed *pactum salutis*, which maintains that the *hypostases*, for the sake of redemption, take on economic roles that they did not previously have. Cf. ibid., 75.

23. Ibid., 75–76.

awareness of this distinctness in one only real consciousness."[24] A single divine consciousness exists, though the three persons possess it in a different way.[25] There is only one "person" in the Godhead, according to Rahner's working philosophical definition of "person."[26] Notwithstanding, in a creedal sense, there are three. Having defined *hypostases* to this degree, Rahner must then relate the *hypostases* to each other. Traditionally, this has been done by the doctrine of *perichoresis*.

Relating the Persons of the Trinity

Many different versions of *perichoresis* have been developed in contemporary Christianity.[27] Athanasius and the Cappadocian Fathers developed the earliest form of the doctrine between the ecumenical councils of Nicaea and Constantinople, and the Athanasian Creed presented a form that Anselm developed further.[28] *Perichoresis* is the coinherence of each *hypostasis* with the divine essence and therefore with the other *hypostases*. This doctrine is intended to explain how unity and diversity can exist simultaneously in the Godhead without resorting to a form of dialecticism. If misunderstood, it can blur the distinctions

24. Ibid., 107.

25. Rahner appeals to Bernard Lonergan for support on this point. See ibid., 107n21.

26. Ibid., 107n30.

27. See, for instance, Catherine Mowry LaCugna, *God for Us: The Trinity and Christian Life* (San Francisco: HarperSanFrancisco, 1991), 270–78; Herman Bavinck, *Reformed Dogmatics*, vol. 2, *God and Creation* (Grand Rapids: Baker Academic, 2004), 298–304; Charles Hodge, *Systematic Theology* (Peabody, MA: Hendrickson, 1999), 1:461–62; Richard A. Muller, *Post-Reformation Reformed Dogmatics: The Rise and Development of Reformed Orthodoxy, ca. 1520 to ca. 1725*, vol. 4, *The Triunity of God*, 2nd ed. (Grand Rapids: Baker Academic, 2003), 57, 185, 186.

28. For a useful account of this history, see, J. N. D. Kelly, *Early Christian Doctrines* (San Francisco: HarperSanFrancisco, 1978), 263ff.; Anselm, *Monologion*, §59. See also Sandra Visser and Thomas Williams, *Anselm*, Great Medieval Thinkers (Oxford, New York: Oxford University Press, 2009), 146; Muller, *Post-Reformation Reformed Dogmatics*, 4:57.

between the *hypostases* (Sabellianism) or posit three distinct Gods (tritheism).

The Father is unbegotten, the Son is begotten, and the Spirit proceeds. These particular modes of subsistence have come to define the distinctions among the *hypostases* for the Western tradition.[29] If a distinction is not maintained at every point, the *hypostases* become changing modes of existence or mere presentations of the divine essence. If separation is introduced at any point, division or multiplication of the divine essence occurs, resulting in each *hypostasis* having its own essence. In effect, each *hypostasis* would be a god unto itself. Rahner is aware of these dangers, especially as he considers the possibility of three distinct consciousnesses in the Godhead.[30] For Rahner, divine consciousness and essence are closely linked, such that multiplying consciousnesses entails multiplying essences. This would be highly problematic, since a plurality of essences results in polytheism. The error of Sabellianism is equally dangerous. If the orthodox theologian cannot deny the existence of three persons in the Godhead, he must struggle constantly in his Trinitarian formulations with the tension between the creedal use of "persons" to describe the diversity within the Godhead and a contemporary understanding of "subjectivity." But the problem is that these two are so closely related that the creedal formulations are inevitably colored by the notion of subjectivity.[31]

29. See, for example, Bavinck, *Reformed Dogmatics*, 2:304ff.; Muller, *Post-Reformation Reformed Dogmatics*, 4:50ff.

30. "There can be no doubt about it: speaking of three persons in God entails almost inevitably the danger (as a rule we try much too late to overcome it through explicit connections) of believing that there exist in God three distinct consciousnesses, spiritual vitalities, centers of activity, and so on" (Rahner, *The Trinity*, 43).

31. "If someone today, whether Christian or not, hears the statement that there are three persons in God, he will think instinctively of three subjects differing from one another in their subjectivity, knowledge, and freedom, and wonder what kind of

Rahner recognizes this, and he expresses his concern that the traditional Boethian understanding of personhood, when applied to the Trinity, requires the multiplication of the divine essence as well as the centers of mental action ("consciousnesses"). According to a Boethian understanding, if there are three persons, there must also be three subsistences in the rational nature. Yet this is unnecessarily complicated for Rahner,[32] and to counteract this misunderstanding, he subjects the hypostatic relations to the divine unity in his formulation of *perichoresis*. In Rahner's view, this protects monotheism and opens avenues for ecumenical dialogue with Jews and Muslims. There is one God, one consciousness, one will, and, philosophically speaking, one person.

Conclusion

As Rahner explores how God is a person, he navigates several important theological topics. Beginning with the human experience of the ineffable divine mystery, Rahner explicates a definition of *hypostasis* that is grounded in the Father as unoriginate and the Son and Spirit as the twofold divine self-communication to humanity in transcendental and categorical experience. Now by turning to theological anthropology, we may gather a richer understanding of Trinitarian personhood from within Rahner's theological context.

---

logic it is that permits three persons understood in this way to be simultaneously one and the same God. Even if this modern man uses the definition of official textbook theology, that personality is the subsistence of a rational nature, and if he is told that the rational nature need not be increased numerically in line with the plurality of subsistences, he is still in danger of thinking of the rationality of these subsistences as sharing their plurality, of thinking of them as three reciprocally related centres of mental action, related to one another as such" (Rahner, "Oneness and Threefoldness of God in Discussion with Islam," 110–11).

32. Rahner, "Oneness and Threefoldness of God in Discussion with Islam," 111.

3

THE RECIPIENTS OF GRACE

Within Rahner's theology, theological anthropology has about as much to say about God's being as does theology proper. God communicates nothing less than himself to human beings, who are created specifically to receive this gift of self; therefore, the very fabric of man's nature discloses the characteristics of the God who desires to give himself to them.[1] This basic starting point is in essence a matter of personality and interpersonal relationships. It is a thread woven throughout Rahner's theology and philosophy, especially his theology of grace.

The Nature of Man

The Historical Beginnings of Rahner's Anthropology

Because of their occasional nature and pastoral focus, most of Rahner's extant writings are anthropological, but two early works crystallize his basic anthropological concerns. The first of

---

1. "The Trinity is a mystery whose paradoxical character is preluded in the paradoxical character of man's existence" (Karl Rahner, *The Trinity* [New York: Crossroad, 1997], 47).

these was published in 1939 as *Geist in Welt* (*Spirit in the World*). In it, Rahner studies Aquinas's *Summa Theologiae* I, q. 84, a. 7, which explores whether the intellect may understand something completely and truly without resorting to the process of abstraction through sense perception.[2] From this starting point, Rahner develops a transcendental metaphysics of epistemology. The other significant anthropological work of this time was *Hörer des Wortes* (*Hearers of the Word*), the first edition of which appeared in 1941.[3] J. B. Metz, one of Rahner's best-known students, edited a revised edition of this book in 1963.[4] *Hörer des Wortes* was written early in Rahner's theological career, near to the time of his mandatory Jesuit philosophical training. Although he did not abandon his philosophical concerns in later years, his earlier writings are much more philosophical in character, while his later works are often more practical and pastoral. *Hörer des Wortes* was also published during the Second World War, a tumultuous time of transition for Rahner. Austria was annexed by Germany in March 1938,

2. The question is "Whether the intellect can actually understand through the intelligible species of which it is possessed, without turning to the phantasms?" Thomas argues, "Wherefore the nature of a stone or any material thing cannot be known completely and truly, except in as much as it is known as existing in the individual. Now we apprehend the individual through the senses and the imagination. And, therefore, for the intellect to understand actually its proper object, it must of necessity turn to the phantasms in order to perceive the universal nature existing in the individual. But if the proper object of our intellect were a separate form; or if, as the Platonists say, the natures of sensible things subsisted apart from the individual; there would be no need for the intellect to turn to the phantasms whenever it understands" (*Summa Theologica* I, q. 84, a. 7, ad 3).

3. Both versions are available in the critical edition of Rahner's works: Karl Rahner, *Sämtliche Werke*, vol. 4, *Hörer de Wortes*, ed. Albert Raffelt (Solothurn, Düsseldorf: Benziger, 1997).

4. Karl Rahner, *Hörer des Wortes: Zur Grundlegung einer Religionsphilosophie*, ed. Johannes Baptist Metz (München: Kösel, 1963). Although Rahner may have worked closely with Metz, significant debate persists among scholars as to whether the first edition should be preferred to Metz's revision. See, for example, Thomas Sheehan, *Karl Rahner: The Philosophical Foundations* (Athens, OH: Ohio University Press, 1987), 11–12.

and the government closed the school of theology at Innsbruck. From 1938 until 1944, Rahner was associated with the pastoral office in Vienna. He lectured unofficially for Jesuit students of the University of Vienna while these courses were given at a Benedictine monastery away from the government's view.[5] It was a transitional time early in his career, and these works, perhaps more than his later works, should be read with special attention given to his early personal-intellectual and national-political context.

A Twofold Nature

Rahner believes man possesses a twofold nature, characterized as spiritual and historical. These twin aspects underscore and orient the dynamism of human existence and inform all aspects of Rahner's theology and theological methodology. For this reason, Rahner begins *Hearers of the Word* by locating his enquiry between the two "sciences" of theology and philosophy of religion. The subject matter of theology is divine revelation, a communication originating outside the natural world. This distinguishes theology from philosophy of religion, which obtains "the knowledge which man is *on his own* able to acquire of the correct relation of man to God as Absolute."[6] While they are based on different *principia*, both are necessary. These two sciences correspond to man's twofold nature. The transcendent spiritual aspect is receptive to divine revelation, and the concrete historical aspect operates according to man's natural faculties. The two are complementary and explore equally constitutive aspects of man's existence.

---

5. For a lengthier treatment, see Karl H. Neufeld, *Die Brüder Rahner: Eine Biographie* (Freiburg: Herder, 1994), 159–76.

6. Karl Rahner, *Hearers of the Word*, ed. Johannes Baptist Metz, trans. Michael Richards (New York: Herder and Herder, 1969), 7. A translation of the first edition by Joseph Donceel, edited by Andew Tallon, is entitled *Hearer of the Word* (New York: Continuum, 1994). The German word *Hörer* can be either singular or plural.

Each human being lives in the world according to his natural capacity, but always with the possibility of hearing from someone beyond this world. He is a spirit in the world and a transcendent hearer of the word, dependent on God and constituted by an ability and readiness to receive his revelation.[7] This dynamic relation informs us of both man's ability and the character of God's communication. Because man exists in history, God's communication to him must also have a history, one that is constituted and established whether or not God chooses to reveal himself. Man is always related to God, either as the recipient of his revelation or as the capable one waiting for it.[8] The possibility is always present. By describing the relationship in this way, Rahner is able to preserve divine freedom while also retaining the capacity for divine communication as a meaningful and constitutive part of man's nature.

Man is the divinely created recipient of God's communication. In Rahner's writings, this capacity is known as man's *obediential potency*. God and man belong together. Nonetheless, it cannot be the case that God *needs* man. Nor could it be the case for Rahner that human beings must respond to God. If humans were required to respond to God in a deterministic manner, the relationship could not be a genuinely personal exchange characterized by thought, emotion, and especially freedom. To address this difficulty, Rahner links man's constitutive nature to the *potential* of hearing from God, rather than to the actual reception of God's self-communication. Divine freedom, rather than divine self-communication, grounds human existence, because man is fundamentally oriented toward the divine mystery, whether or not God actually communicates himself.

7. Rahner, *Hearers of the Word*, 16.
8. "Should God, of his free choice, wish not to reveal himself but to remain silent, man would attain the ultimate and highest self-perfection of his spiritual and religious existence by listening to the silence of God" (ibid., 16).

We start to see how personality flows through every aspect of Rahner's ontology. Both aspects of man's nature involve freedom, which itself presupposes agency and therefore personality. Just as divine freedom constitutes human existence in its transcendent, spiritual aspect, so also human freedom conditions the concrete historical component of man's existence. Human existence is characterized by personal freedom exercised in the face of God's personal self-communication. History in turn is the record and context of man's free response to God's self-communication.[9] Both parties always retain the personal integrity of freedom.[10] They can have a genuinely interpersonal relationship of mutual giving and receiving. Whether or not he accepts God's free offer, man acts as a personal agent making decisions of interpersonal consequence.

General Ontology

Again, Rahner is concerned most of all with describing how God communicates himself to mankind. To answer this question, one must know something about created being in general, since general ontology provides the concrete context in which historical man lives and moves. This may be the most challenging aspect of Rahner's theology for those not steeped in Thomistic and Heideggerian metaphysics to understand. The divine-human relationship is transcendent and spiritual, but it

---

9. "Man is historical insofar as he is the one who acts in a freedom that originates in his transcendence with respect to God, that is, according to the determination of his relationship to the absolute" (ibid., 133).

10. For Rahner, "freedom is not simply the capacity to do this or that but (formally) a *self*-disposing into finality; the subject (from a formal point of view) is always concerned with itself" (Karl Rahner, "Reflections on the Unity of the Love of Neighbour and the Love of God," in *Theological Investigations*, edited by Karl-H. Kruger and Boniface Kruger, vol. 6 [London: Darton, Longman & Todd, 1969], 240).

occurs in the world.[11] Earthly phenomena and the interpersonal relationships in it are the media through which man experiences God. According to Rahner, "The essence of being is knowing and being known in an original unity."[12] This characterizes the exchange between divine and human persons as one of agency and knowledge. In other words, knowledge is more than intellectual data; it is relational and personal. Human beings are unique among beings that belong to general ontology, because humans are concrete beings who transcend concreteness by questioning their own existence.[13]

Rahner proposes a unity of spirit and matter, body and soul, which allows for knowledge to come from within. Following Aquinas, he recognizes that the intellect takes an active role in abstraction and the formulation of judgments regarding the sensible world.[14] Rahner's method for explaining this complex structure is heavily influenced by the Belgian Jesuit Joseph Maréchal, whose insights led Rahner to his transcendental interpretation of Aquinas. While this influence set the stage for Rahner's later work, it also led to the failure of his dissertation, which eventually became *Geist in Welt*.[15] In this work, Rahner develops a

11. "This is already seen to be true by the fact that the true and proper surrounding of man is his personal environment. This environment of persons is the world through which man finds and fulfils himself (by knowledge and will) and . . . gets away from himself" (ibid., 240).

12. "The essence of being is knowing and being known in an original unity, which we call the (conscious) being-present-to-itself of being. Expressing this in terms of modern philosophy we would say: the being of that existent being which is self-illuminating. Being is illuminated in itself" (Rahner, *Hearers of the Word*, 39–40.) Further, "The nature of being is knowing and being known in their original unity. In other words, being present to itself and self-luminosity" (ibid., 38).

13. "Not until we come to man does the expression of his specific essence in thought and action return for the first time to itself. In showing, by thought and deed, what he is, man knows about himself" (ibid., 50).

14. Robert Pasnau, *Theories of Cognition in the Later Middle Ages* (Cambridge, New York: Cambridge University Press, 1997), 129.

15. Rahner studied philosophy at Freiburg under Martin Honecker, but also

transcendental metaphysics of epistemology that is present throughout his writings, even occupying significant portions of his later work.

Rahner identifies a significant problem posed by his twofold understanding of man: How can we come to know about the reality that *transcends* the world, if we live as concrete beings *within* the world? Moreover, how can we know *anything* outside of ourselves, if our knowledge is fundamentally self-presence, that is, being present to one's self (*Beisichsein*)?[16] These questions reveal that, to Rahner, man is inescapably part of the sensible world. Man needs some way to escape himself in order to "know." Rahner solves this problem by understanding knowledge as self-presence. To have knowledge of a sensible object—that is, something external to the mind and accessible through the senses—is to exist somehow with the being of that object while also remaining distinct from it.[17] Human beings have the unique ability to do this.

God transcends the world. Man is in the world, but can also transcend it. God can speak to man by "encoding" his absolute

---

attended seminars under Martin Heidegger. His dissertation was titled *Geist in Welt: Zur Metaphysik der endlichen Erkenntnis bei Thomas von Aquin*. Honecker rejected Rahner's transcendental interpretation of Thomas and subsequently failed this dissertation. Surprisingly, Rahner later confessed that he was not bothered by what others would consider devastating. He was relieved that his failure would allow him to focus on theology instead. See Harvey Egan, *Karl Rahner: Mystic of Everyday Life* (New York: Crossroad, 1998), 14, 22.

16. Karen Kilby condenses the epistemological concerns of *Spirit in the World* into two brief questions: "The initial and most basic question of *Spirit in the World* is 'how is metaphysics possible given that all our knowledge is grounded in the world?'" And second, "If all our knowledge starts with and remains enmeshed with the world of time and space, the world known through the senses, how is it that we can nevertheless know that which surpasses time and space and sense perception?" (Karen Kilby, *Karl Rahner: Theology and Philosophy* [London, New York: Routledge, 2004], 17).

17. See Winfred George Phillips, "Rahner's Transcendental Deduction of the *Vorgriff*," *The Thomist* 56 (1992): 258; Sheehan, *Karl Rahner*, 161–68; Kilby, *Karl Rahner*, 2004, 15–19.

essence to man, and people can receive it, because they possess as part of their nature the code—the instructions—for understanding and receiving this communication. Revelation, therefore, teaches us about man's origin and purpose. God created mankind so that he could communicate to us through revelation; therefore, human experience is fundamental, not only to theological anthropology, but also to metaphysics and ontology in general.[18]

For all of this to work, man needs a reference point. If the intellect is to emanate sensibility and exist with the being of the object it perceives, there must be some background or context against which this object can be understood. When man reaches out to this context in transcendence, he exhibits a *Vorgriff auf esse*, a "pre-apprehension of being."[19] The *Vorgriff* makes sensible knowledge possible by providing the necessary context for understanding the particulars. When man's spirit emanates sensibility, it is present with the other object, which it seeks to know. To understand this concrete particular, the human spirit must not only recognize it, but also situate it within the entire horizon of being. Throughout his writings, Rahner is not clear as to what specifically is apprehended by the *Vorgriff*. In *Spirit in the World*, he argues that the *Vorgriff* is not a pre-apprehension of "a humanly conceivable object," but he also recognizes that it cannot reach

---

18. Thomas Sheehan affirms this unique aspect of Rahner's approach: "If man is intrinsically the movement beyond (*meta*) beings (*ta physika*) to their beingness (*eis physin*), that is, if he is the concrete and worldly differentiation of beings and their beingness, then the thematic discipline called metaphysics is not a flight to heaven but a worldly hermeneutics (*hermēneia, Auslegen*) which merely lays out—i.e., brings to light, appropriates, and articulates—the knowledge man already has. Indeed, it is only the conceptually formulated understanding of that prior understanding which man as man *is*" (*Karl Rahner: The Philosophical Foundations* [Athens, OH: Ohio University Press, 1987], 158).

19. "This transcending apprehension of further possibilities, through which the form possessed in a concretion in sensibility is apprehended as limited and so is abstracted, we call 'pre-apprehension' ('*Vorgriff*')" (Karl Rahner, *Spirit in the World*, trans. William Dych [New York: Herder and Herder, 1968], 142).

out to "nothing," since that would render it useless.[20] Having a pre-apprehension of being, then, man is able to recognize the limit of each individual sensible thing he encounters. He can thereby understand how it relates to the entire context of knowledge and, finally, God's being itself. Without this *Vorgriff*, such a recognition or comparison could not take place. The *Vorgriff* is the *a priori* context for *a posteriori* knowledge.

Grace: A Personal Relationship

Free Recipients of Grace

All human beings have a sense of the grace that God offers to them. This grace is a fundamental aspect, even a constituent element, of human existence.[21] Rahner calls this aspect of human existence the "supernatural existential," since an "existential," as understood by Rahner, is something common to all human experience, not simply one particular experience.[22] Human beings are fundamentally open to a self-communication from God, whether or not they have thematized that experience.[23] God is free to offer himself or refrain from doing so, and human beings

20. Rahner, *Spirit in the World*, 143–45. Rahner himself asked, "Is this horizon that of the imagination of infinite space and time, or is it broader, in principle unlimited in every dimension, the horizon of being absolutely, which thus discloses itself as transcending space and time?" (ibid., 143).

21. Karen Kilby, "Rahner," in *The Blackwell Companion to Modern Theology*, ed. Gareth Jones (Malden, MA: Blackwell, 2004), 348.

22. Ibid., 345.

23. Karen Kilby offers a helpful explanation: "Closely related to the *Vorgriff*, but at least theoretically to be distinguished from it, is the 'supernatural existential.' Just as Rahner maintains that there is a universal apprehension of God, so he also holds that there is a universal experience of grace, or at least of grace as offered, and this he calls the supernatural existential. In the theory of the supernatural existential we have another claim of universal scope: it is a theory of the nature of everyone's deepest experience, which is also a theory of the relation of nature to grace, and which is closely linked to Rahner's understanding of revelation, Christology and salvation" (ibid.).

are also free to accept or reject the offer. This constitutes a truly personal relationship. Rahner calls this basic existential decision a "fundamental option," that is, a primordial decision that occurs unthematically. It is therefore possible for someone to reach out to God as the ineffable mystery without at the same time possessing thematized rational reflection upon that decision. This is the kernel of Rahner's doctrine of the anonymous Christian, and it is congruent with the idea that God's self-communication is available universally.

Created and Uncreated Grace

Traditionally, Roman Catholics have conceived of grace as a created gift given to balance out man's inclination toward self-love. To counteract this inclination, God endowed man with a *donum superadditum*, a super-added gift. Man lost this supernatural endowment at the fall. To overcome this deficiency, grace is now given through the sacraments. Rahner does not reject this traditional understanding, but he does choose to emphasize another form of grace, following the Scholastics, who distinguished between created and uncreated grace. Whereas created grace is a divine quality given to mankind originally in the *donum superadditum* and then through the sacraments, uncreated grace is personal union and communion with God himself—a *donum increatum*.[24] Rahner recognized a problem with Scholastic

24. Karl Rahner, "Some Implications of the Scholastic Concept of Uncreated Grace," in *Theological Investigations*, trans. Cornelius Ernst, vol. 1 (Baltimore: Helicon, 1969), 322. Daniel Donovan offers a helpful summary of Rahner's concerns: "Following Aquinas Rahner saw grace as the key to Christianity. Whereas the tradition before him primarily understood it as a created reality, a disposition of the human spirit enabling it through faith, hope, and love to be in an intimate relationship with God, Rahner emphasized what the tradition had called uncreated grace. Grace, in this sense, is God turned to us, inviting and enabling us to share the divine life, drawing us into a dynamic and dialogical relationship with himself" (Daniel Donovan, "Revelation and Faith," in *The Cambridge Companion to Karl Rahner*, ed. Declan Marmion and Mary E. Hines [Cambridge: Cambridge University Press, 2005], 85).

theology. Human beings only exist in communion with God after they receive created grace. In other words, human beings *as created* have no inherent relationship to God. More than that, God cannot communicate or dwell with humans unless they receive created grace. Rahner is so concerned with divine self-communication that his soteriology, as well as his anthropology, is based upon it.

According to Rahner, the problem with the Scholastics' dominant view of soteriology is that they "see God's indwelling and his conjunction with the justified man as based exclusively upon created grace."[25] Man is *created* to receive God's communication, whether or not he has received or lost the *donum superadditum*. That cannot be the case for the Scholastics. Man is natural—in a sense, neutral—and needs a special gift for him to be positively related to God and receive God's gift of self. Rahner rejects that ordering, because the very nature of humanity is to be able to receive God's self-communication, regardless of created grace. Uncreated grace cannot be a subsequent blessing; it needs to be the essence of God's relationship with mankind either before or after the fall into sin: "Thus on our view of the relationship between created and uncreated grace there does not exist even the beginning of a possibility of thinking of created grace apart from uncreated grace, and so of thinking of uncreated grace as a fresh gift arising out of a new and independent demonstration of God's grace."[26] The gift of God's Spirit is based on "an absolute entitative modification of man himself,"[27] which is independent of created grace and even the fall into sin.

God's desire to communicate himself to man precedes—logically and temporally—the outcome of man's initial probation.

---

25. Rahner, "Some Implications of the Scholastic Concept of Uncreated Grace," 324.
26. Ibid., 341.
27. Ibid., 324.

In order to explain this feature of his theology of grace, Rahner turns his attention to the Catholic distinction between healing and elevating grace. Healing grace refers to the process of sanctification, that is, the restoration needed as a result of sin. Healing grace is predicated upon the difference between good and evil. Elevating grace, however, is the grace given to bring man to an estate higher than the one in which he was created. It is predicated upon the difference between good and perfected. Elevating grace is not properly soteriological, but protological, that is, relative to the original ordering of creation. Elevating grace is also eschatological, because it moves mankind toward a divinely intended consummation. The gift of uncreated grace, then, is related to the gift of elevating grace. Through the indwelling of the Holy Spirit, the spiritual subject is transformed and eventually brought to consummation. The entire movement of human history has been directed toward the basic idea that God desires to give himself to human beings by means of a personal, ontological, and historical communication of self.

Encountering the Trinity

Rahner's doctrine of grace has significant implications for his Trinitarian theology and vice versa. Since it is *Trinitarian* self-communication, grace must demonstrate the characteristics of its intended recipient in order for it to be meaningful.[28] The Trinity is the basic reality of God's existence, but it is also the means by which God is able to communicate himself to the

28. Karen Kilby helpfully describes the character of this self-communication: "What we learn from revelation in the more ordinary sense of the word, from Christianity as a historical religion, from the Old and New Testaments, is not something simply new and previously unknown, not something that comes from outside and is unconnected with our experience. What is given is rather a thematization of that which is already experienced in our innermost depths. Revelation then is not primarily a set of truths, a God-given extension of our ordinary knowledge, but God's

twofold nature of man. The being of God and the being of man are related; all ontology is principally concerned with this divine-human personal relationship.

The Trinity Revealed

In accord with his basic Trinitarian axiom, Rahner maintains that the Trinity humans know is the Trinity which has been revealed. From a human perspective, God communicates himself transcendentally, but he always does so in conjunction with categorical revelation, in language and events, because this revelation must be made concrete in the world and history.[29] The goal of this self-communication, which will be addressed further in the next chapter, is the divinization of the creature. While this is strong theological language, Rahner does not intend to compromise the integrity of either the divine or the human nature.[30] For our immediate concerns, let us affirm that Rahner is able to relate man directly to the Trinity through a personal relationship without compromising intra-Trinitarian relations, the distinct personal properties of each *hypostasis*, or the Creator-creature distinction.

The Trinity Experienced

Because God transcends creation, we may be tempted to consider him abstractly, more as an idea than a personal existent. Rahner emphasizes that while God transcends the world, the Trinity is also experienced in the world. Humans meet God in their present lives; they are not merely waiting to meet him

---

giving of *himself*, the divine self-communication to the human being in the supernatural existential" (*Karl Rahner*, 56).

29. Ibid., 141n20. See also Karl Rahner, *Foundations of Christian Faith: An Introduction to the Idea of Christianity* (New York: Seabury, 1978), 173.

30. Rahner, "Some Implications of the Scholastic Concept of Uncreated Grace," 346.

in some eschatological future. The Trinity is not revealed as an abstract entity. It is revealed in history to men with concrete existence; therefore, human beings must experience Trinitarian self-communication through the media of this world. Some theologians might take this seed and plant it in the soil of paganism or pantheism, but Rahner uses it to develop a practical and ecclesiological theology within the larger context of his general ontology. Beginning with the two great commandments (Matt. 22:37–40) and then developing several Johannine passages, Rahner establishes a fundamental unity between love of God and love of neighbor.[31] The two are coterminous and simultaneous in Rahner's view, since the Trinity is experienced and enjoyed when human beings love their neighbors. Charity (*caritas*) is meaningful in its own right. It does not lose its identity by being dissolved into the love of God. Nonetheless, true charity—love of neighbor—can never be isolated from the love of God: "The one does not exist and cannot be understood or exercised without the other."[32] Rahner is concerned that contemporary philosophy moves people to think of God as a mystery that can be known and experienced only in some future reality beyond the world of present human experience.[33] Such a view is problematic to Rahner, who is eager to maintain the genuineness of divine self-communication even within present human experience. His theology, then, in the strictest sense, is *practical* theology.[34] As human beings live in the world and interact lovingly with those around them, they encounter other spirits in the world who likewise are capable of receiving divine self-communication. Indeed, they encounter the triune God himself.

31. Rahner, "Reflections on the Unity of the Love of Neighbour and the Love of God," 232.

32. Ibid., 232.

33. Ibid., 232–33.

34. Ibid., 233.

Although love of God and love of neighbor coincide, there is a proper ordering. Love of God precedes and is foundational to love of neighbor. Even though prayer and trust are directed immediately toward God,[35] there is a more basic ontological reason why love of God is primary. God's love evokes a response from the free subject. His gracious self-communication, an act of love, is the horizon upon which all human actions take place. Love of neighbor must then be understood through the transcendental and categorical grid of human acts. When one free human subject engages in an act of loving his or her neighbor, the free subject acts categorically in the concrete act,[36] yet that same act has a transcendental aspect directed toward the divine mystery, which is the ultimate horizon or background of free human existence. Grace is always experienced through concrete acts of charity, because these categorical acts always reach out toward the transcendental goal of human existence, namely, acceptance of divine self-communication in grace.[37]

The most fundamental finite act that has transcendental significance as love for God is an act of love for neighbor. This

35. Ibid., 238.

36. This language may sound quite foreign to confessionally Reformed ears. For Rahner, humans can operate according to two dimensions that loosely parallel Kant's noumenal and phenomenal, though with an existentialist influence. Rahner uses the word "categorical" in a way that is similar to Kant's phenomenal categories. These acts of love toward neighbor in this world are done against the horizon of the ineffable mystery. The larger point is that Rahner sees a connection between these dimensions. Although God is transcendent and ultimately beyond this world of experience, he is the horizon behind any action in this life. No matter how a photographer may frame the landscape, the horizon is there in the background, providing its setting and context.

37. "The act of personal love for another human being is therefore the all-embracing basic act of man which gives meaning, direction and measure to everything else. If this is correct, then the essential *a priori* openness to the other human being which must be undertaken freely belongs as such to the *a priori* and most basic constitution of man and is an essential inner moment of his (knowing and willing) transcendentality. This *a priori* basic constitution (which must be accepted

substructure of personal relationships is the basic and constitutive reality for humans. *Personal* love is the interpretive key to human existence. It must be a part of universal human experience regardless of thematic or explicit religious expression. Although he recognizes that this view is not commonly held in Catholic theology, Rahner unites love of neighbor and love of God universally and indiscriminately for human experience. That is, all human beings experience it, not only the redeemed: "Wherever there is an absolutely moral commitment of a positive kind in the world and within the present economy of salvation, there takes place also a saving event, faith, hope and charity, an act of divinising grace, and thus *caritas* is exercised in this."[38] This is the kernel of Rahner's doctrine of the "anonymous Christian." It is important to recognize that his theological formulation presupposes his general ontology and theological anthropology. Outside this personal ontological context, his conclusion seems pluralistic and even irrational, but given the underlying features of Rahner's theological anthropology, in conjunction with the triune God's universal offer of grace, his "anonymous Christianity" is not merely plausible, but the necessary conclusion. A saving

---

in freedom, but to which man can also close himself) is experienced in the concrete encounter with man in the concrete" (Rahner, "Reflections on the Unity of the Love of Neighbour and the Love of God," 241). Rahner continues, "The one moral (or immoral) basic act in which man comes to himself and decides basically about himself is also the (loving or hating) communication with the concrete Thou in which man experiences, accepts or denies his basic *a priori* reference to the Thou as such. Everything else is a factor in this or a consequence of it or an impulse towards it, but in the present order of salvation, i.e., one having a supernatural goal, *this basic* act is, according to what has been said, elevated supernaturally by a self-communication of God in uncreated grace and in the resulting basic triune faculty of the theological virtues of faith, hope and charity, whereby theological love necessarily and of its very nature integrates and saves faith and hope into itself. Hence the one basic human act, where it takes place positively, is the love of neighbour understood as *caritas*, i.e., as a love of neighbour whose movement is directed towards the God of eternal life" (ibid., 241).

38. Ibid., 239.

experience of the triune God is not predicated on thematic or explicit religious experience. The question is not first and foremost, "Are you a Catholic?" It is, "Are you a human being?"

Conclusion

Rahner's Trinitarian theology and theological anthropology are bound together by a thoroughly personal atmosphere that serves as the medium through which man's twofold nature is expressed. Humans reach out through the *Vorgriff*, but never reach God in the sense that they can possess him. He always remains an ineffable mystery. In that sense, the divine-human relationship is asymptotic. Much like repeatedly dividing a number in half brings the result closer and closer to zero without ever reaching zero, the free subject reaches out more and more, but never fully arrives at the divine mystery. If God's self-communication is to be fully realized, there must be a climactic divine gift of self equally matched by an irrevocable acceptance of that gift. Such is the case in the hypostatic union.

4

HYPOSTATIC UNION
AND PERSONALITY

Our overarching theme has been that the triune God creates man as the intended recipient of divine self-communication, the Trinitarian gift of self. Man is a spirit in history, who is always confronted with the free offer of divine grace (self-communication). The succession of these individual personal choices to accept or reject God's offer is the essence of history. God's repeated offer to humanity in time is consummated in the person of Jesus Christ, because the hypostatic union of divine and human natures in the person of the Son is the fullest and perfect instance of the divine offer and its human acceptance. Jesus Christ, the God-man, is the new humanity, the apex of history.

To understand Rahner's formulation of the hypostatic union, we must understand its lineage. Rahner began with a traditional understanding of the doctrine formulated at the Council of Chalcedon and explicated by Thomas Aquinas. This was merely the starting block from which he would launch into a Christology for his contemporary era. By comparing and contrasting Aquinas and Rahner on the hypostatic union, we will be able to continue our analysis of Trinitarian personality. God communicates himself to human beings climactically in the hypostatic union. Christology completes theology proper and anthropology. Only after closing this loop may we return to the starting point of Rahner's Trinitarian axiom by way of soteriology as we see the significance of the hypostatic union for the whole of humanity.

The Thomistic Context of Twentieth-Century Catholicism

We will begin with the theological context that led up to the Second Vatican Council, where Rahner's theology began to flourish. Few theologians have had such enduring influence as Thomas Aquinas, which is especially true for twentieth-century Catholicism. Aquinas's works have stood the test of time and continue to influence Catholics and Protestants alike. One of his greatest contributions to Christian theology was his rigorous treatment of Christology, which, in his analysis, centered on the Chalcedonian creed. The Council of Chalcedon, convened in 451, affirmed the virgin birth and formulated the creedal statement that Christ is one person with two natures inseparably united, yet distinct. Aquinas provided a metaphysical account for the Chalcedonian formula. He sought to define precisely how the eternal Son of God could take to himself a true human nature and become one person with two distinct natures. His treatment continues to be influential today.

Leo XIII established the philosophy of Thomas Aquinas as the official position of the Roman Catholic Church in 1879, and in 1910 Pius X required subscription to an antimodernist oath for ordination.[1] For several decades, it was practically impossible to find a Catholic theologian in good standing who would not call himself a Thomist. Karl Rahner was no exception. Having studied Thomist philosophy for three years as part of the standard Jesuit training of the day, Rahner became very familiar with Thomism—particularly the neo-Thomist variety. Rahner was not alone in seeing Aquinas as a historical figure who could speak into the present.[2] Many were dissatisfied with the reigning neo-Thomism and opted to refashion the theology of Aquinas. Seeking a venue for theological creativity, these thinkers swept up Aquinas in their own version of Kant's turn to the subject.[3] What is now known as transcendental Thomism refashioned Aquinas without transgressing the Pope's declaration of 1879

1. Darrell Jodock, ed., *Catholicism Contending with Modernity: Roman Catholic Modernism and Anti-Modernism in Historical Context* (Cambridge: Cambridge University Press, 2000), 7.

2. "When Rahner spoke of being a student of Thomas Aquinas and a Thomist, which he always claimed to be, he said that it was his own questions arising out of the present that prompted him to read the past. He wanted to interpret Aquinas not just as an historian would whose interest was the past, but as a philosopher concerned with the present, and always keeping an eye on the reality Thomas was talking about. Confronting the insights of Thomas with modern philosophy and its questions yields yet deeper insight into both. By this process of cross-fertilization classical philosophy of the Western tradition beginning with the Greeks, the *philosophia perennis*, remains a living truth addressing the present and does not become a dead letter of the past" (William V. Dych, *Karl Rahner* [Collegeville MN: Liturgical Press, 1992], 2).

3. Two early key figures in this transcendental shift in Thomistic interpretation were Pierre Rousselot and Joseph Maréchal. They paved a way for Rahner and others, who came later. Gerald McCool described the theological *Zeitgeist*: "Thomist historians of philosophy, like Etienne Gilson, were convinced that they could identify the authentic Christian Philosophy of the Angelic Doctor and determine its proper relation to theology. Maréchalian Thomists still believed that, by using the transcendental method, they could overcome Kantian idealism from within. By doing so, they could vindicate the Angelic Doctor's metaphysics of being, potency and act as the genuine metaphysics of man and being" (Gerald McCool, "Karl Rahner and the Christian Philosophy of St. Thomas Aquinas," in *Theology and Discovery: Essays in Honor of Karl Rahner, S.J.*, edited by William J. Kelly [Milwaukee: Marquette University Press, 1980], 71.)

or the antimodernist oath. This new formulation became successful to the degree that it may have obviated itself.[4] The significance of this creative interpretation began to fade after the Second Vatican Council set out an aggressive agenda to update the Roman Catholic Church for a contemporary setting. In its wake, the antimodernist oath was dropped in 1967, and the tenor of the magisterium quickly changed.[5] During the Council, the once nascent transcendental theology grew firm roots. Figures like Rahner, whom the magisterium watched with suspicion just prior to the Council's commencement, now became its foremost authorities.[6] To many, the Roman Catholic Church was turned upside down, and the historical theologians were left to sort out the relationship between the Rome of yesterday and its latest instantiation.

The post-Vatican II Rahner and the medieval Aquinas desired to root their Christological doctrines within an orthodox understanding of Chalcedon. Neither was interested in being considered outside the bounds of the Council's formulation. Still, the transcendental Thomism of Karl Rahner is vastly different from its scholastic forebear. While it could be considered problematic to be at odds with Aquinas, it liberates Rahner to develop his theology of grace. That is, he may present Jesus Christ, the God-man, as the epochal human acceptance of the free offer of

4. The transcendental reading of Thomas Aquinas opened up other ecclesiological and ecumenical avenues. Consequently, the Roman Catholic Church lost much of its exclusivity and became open to other theologies and philosophies. Ironically, the transcendental reading of Thomas, which was used in a clever way to circumvent Rome's narrow views, eventually made itself unnecessary by contributing to the broadening of the church.

5. Arthur L. Kennedy, "Theology in the Nineteenth and Twentieth Centuries: 2. Roman Catholic Theology," in *The Encyclopedia of Christianity*, vol. 5, ed. Erwin Fahlbusch et al., trans. Geoffrey W. Bromiley (Grand Rapids: Eerdmans, 2008), 411.

6. John O'Malley, *What Happened at Vatican II* (Cambridge, MA: Belknap, 2008), 87, 145; Karen Kilby, *Karl Rahner: Theology and Philosophy* (London, New York: Routledge, 2004), xv.

divine self-communication. In so doing, Rahner connects his Trinitarian theology to his anthropology, and he connects their related notions of personality through Christology.

Rahner on Thomas and Chalcedon

The Council of Chalcedon (451) produced the classic confessional statement describing how the two natures of Jesus Christ relate to each other and to his person. It has come to define orthodox Christology. References to the Council of Chalcedon in Aquinas's *Summa Theologiae* are sparse.[7] Nonetheless, much can be drawn from these few references. Aquinas does not attempt to reinvent the Council's language regarding the relations of the two natures to the one person of Christ. He seeks to formulate his doctrine within the accepted bounds of orthodoxy. Rahner too seeks to remain within the bounds of Chalcedonian orthodoxy, and in several places he emphasizes the importance of abiding by the church's tradition.

Rahner thinks Aquinas exemplifies "Catholic Dogma."[8] He called Aquinas's doctrine the "textbook" Christology, while he sought to move beyond the outdated formulations.[9] Rahner's own treatment of the Council presents a challenge to orthodoxy,

---

7. A cursory investigation of an electronic edition of the *Summa Theologiae* shows that Aquinas refers to Chalcedon explicitly only six times (Thomas Aquinas, *Summa Theologica*, Christian Classics Ethereal Library, accessed June 7, 2019, http://www.ccel.org/ccel/aquinas/summa.txt).

8. "All this is Catholic Dogma. If one is not to fall into a false belief or heresy, one must not think of the God-man as if God or his Logos had put on a kind of livery for the purpose of his saving treatment of man, or as if he had disguised himself, as it were, and had given himself merely an external appearance to enable him to show himself in the world. No, Jesus is truly man" (Karl Rahner, "Christology within an Evolutionary View of the World," in *Theological Investigations*, vol. 5, trans. Karl-H. Kruger [Baltimore: Helicon, 1966], 176).

9. Karl Rahner, "Current Problems in Christology," in *Theological Investigations*, vol. 1, 2nd ed., trans. Cornelius Ernst (Baltimore: Helicon, 1965), 190.

and he occasionally affirms what appear to be two compet-
ing doctrinal formulations. He speaks highly of the Council
at times, but all the while he is setting the stage for his larger
Christological program:

> But I think—and this is all I wanted to say—that even loyalty
> to the faith of Chalcedon permits us and obliges us to inquire
> beyond these formulations of classical Christology and to
> search for other more original or at least equally original chris-
> tological statements which are perhaps closer to Scripture or at
> least to the Christology of the synoptic statements, which we
> can understand more readily, which sound more credible, and
> which still yield classical Christology as implicitly contained in
> them. There is no doubt, of course, that many individual ques-
> tions in classical Christology pose problems of their own.[10]

This is a critical point: in Rahner's view, one may still
affirm Chalcedon while recognizing there is more to say about
Christology. Therefore, Rahner begins with Chalcedon and
Aquinas, but reconfigures the latter considerably. To understand
how he does so, we must detail Aquinas's theology—specifically,
his approach to the Council of Chalcedon.

While Rahner found no difficulty in the Chalcedonian creed,
insofar as it goes, he thought it inadequate for the contemporary world. Language about *hypostases*, substances, and natures
was appropriate for the patristic and medieval ages, but not
for expressing a contemporary Christology. Rahner's primary
aim, in his landmark essay "Christology within an Evolutionary
View of the World," is to remedy this situation by bringing
Christology into the present day. In that essay, he identifies two

---

10. Karl Rahner, "Brief Observations on Systematic Christology Today," in
Theological Investigations, vol. 21, trans. Hugh M. Riley (London: Darton, Longman
& Todd, 1988), 232.

types of Christology that are differentiated initially by their respective starting points, but are not necessarily incompatible. A Christology from below begins with humanity. Rahner calls this a "saving history" type of Christology.[11] Alternatively, a Christology from above, a "metaphysical" type, begins with Christ's divinity.[12] Chalcedon, then, should be conceived as a composite of these two types. It is highly metaphysical, even though the development of its ideas comes in the particular context of established categories. Both types of Christology have a place in Christian theology. Since he did not see them as mutually exclusive, Rahner sought to reconceive Christology within an evolutionary view of the world. That is, he worked to advance Christology so that it would be relevant to people holding a contemporary, scientific worldview.

Vatican II's program of *aggiornamento*[13] is then mirrored on a smaller, but no less significant, scale as Rahner transforms Aquinas's classic Christology. For him, the hypostatic union is the climax of God's offer of self-communication and its acceptance by mankind:

> And this is precisely what is meant by hypostatic union. It means this and, properly speaking, nothing else: in the human reality of Jesus, God's absolute saving purpose (the absolute event of God's self-communication to us) is simply, absolutely and irrevocably present; in it is present both the declaration made to us and its acceptance—something effected by God himself, a reality of God himself, unmixed and yet inseparable

---

11. Karl Rahner, "The Two Basic Types of Christology," in *Theological Investigations*, vol. 13, trans. David Bourke (New York: Seabury, 1975), 213.

12. Ibid., 214.

13. *Aggiornamento* is an Italian word meaning "updating." Under the leadership of John XXIII and later Paul VI, the Second Vatican Council met from 1962 to 1965 to "open the windows" of the church to let in the fresh air of change.

and hence irrevocable. This declaration, however, is the pledge of grace to us.[14]

In his person, Christ became the climax of both offer and acceptance in history, and since it cannot be undone, the offer is irrevocable. In Rahner's theology, the hypostatic union must be situated within salvation history for this offer to be a meaningful personal exchange—not merely individually, but also universally or cosmically. In a sense, the hypostatic union is a universal goal of human existence. Indeed, what occurs interior to the human nature in Christ's hypostatic union is the same for all people who accept the free offer of grace given in Christ:

> The Hypostatic Union takes effect interiorly *for* the human nature of the Logos precisely in what, and really only in what, the same theology prescribes for *all* men as their goal and consummation, viz. the direct vision of God enjoyed by Christ's created human soul. This same theology emphasizes the fact that the Incarnation occurred "for the sake of our salvation," that it does not give any real increase in reality and life to the divine nature of the Logos, and that the prerogatives which accrued interiorly to the human reality of Jesus on account of the Hypostatic Union are of the same essential kind as those intended by grace also for other spiritual subjects.[15]

Such a statement brings Rahner's views into sharp contrast with Aquinas's. For Rahner, the hypostatic union in Christ is an advance upon what will happen for all humans who accept God's free offer of grace. Granted, it does bear some measure of uniqueness since it is a climactic instance, but the metaphysical event of

14. Rahner, "Christology within an Evolutionary View of the World," 182–83.
15. Ibid., 180–81.

human nature being personally, and in that sense *hypostatically,* united to God is not unique:

> Hence the thesis towards which we are working purports to show that, even though the Hypostatic Union is in its proper nature a unique event and—when seen in itself—is certainly the highest conceivable event, it is nevertheless an intrinsic factor of the whole process of the bestowal of grace on the spiritual creature in general.[16]

The hypostatic union, properly considered, has only occurred in Christ, yet it is "an intrinsic factor" in God's plan to commune with his people. Rahner further relates the hypostatic union in Christ with that of the rest of humanity:

> Whenever God—by his absolute self-communication—brings about man's self-transcendence into God, in such a way that both these factors form the irrevocable promise made to all men which has already reached its consummation in this man, there we have a hypostatic union. . . . In Christ, God's self-communication takes place basically for all men, and there is "hypostatic union" precisely in so far as this *unsurpassable* self-communication of God "is there" irrevocably in a historically tangible and self-conscious manner.[17]

Whenever God's self-communication "is there," there is a "hypostatic union," since God gives *himself* (a person, i.e., "*hypostasis*") to *other people.* In this sense, Rahner has broadened the meaning of hypostatic union such that it bears very little resemblance to Aquinas's conception.

16. Ibid., 181.
17. Ibid., 182.

But there is another sense in which Rahner speaks about the hypostatic union, one that understands Christ's hypostatic union as a unique metaphysical event. Only in Christ's hypostatic union is a specific human nature united to the Logos. While this is specific to the person of Christ, Rahner intends to allow that singular hypostatic union to have significance for all of humanity. In order to maintain mankind's constitution in Christ, Rahner distinguishes between *union* and *assumption* at this point. He identifies a difference between (1) incarnational union with Christ (hypostatic union broadly conceived), which occurs for all people by virtue of Christ uniting himself to human nature in general, and (2) the hypostatic union (narrowly conceived) between the Son of God and his individual human nature.[18] Therefore, the assumption of our human natures is directly involved with the union of Christ's human nature to the *hypostasis* of the Logos, but the individual human natures of

---

18. It is helpful to note that Rahner distinguishes between the Hypostatic Union proper (capitalized in the English translation) and the "hypostatic union" of God's grace to each individual human nature (as in the broad sense mentioned above). There is no such distinction in capitalization in the German text. Rahner makes a distinction between Christ's hypostatic union and "hypostatic union" as it happens in each individual human by using Latin with reference to the latter. "Denn eben in uns ist diese Mitteilung möglich und bewirkt durch diese Einigung und Annahme, wie sie in der **hypostatischen Union** geschieht. Und es steht theologisch auf jeden Fall der Annahme nichts im Wege, daß Gnade und **unio hypostatica** nur zusammen gedacht warden können und al seine *Einheit* den einen *freien* Entschluß Gottes zur übernatürlichen Heilsordnung bedeuten. In Christus geschieht die Selbstmitteinlung Gottes grundsätzlich an alle Menschen, und eben insofern diese *unüberbietbare* Selbstmitteilung Gottes in einer unwiderruflichen Weise geschichtlich greifbar und zu sich selbst gekommen 'da ist', ist **unio hypostatica** [italics original; bold italic added]" (Karl Rahner, "Die Christologie innerhalb evolutiver Weltanschauung," in *Sämtliche Werke*, vol. 15, *Verantwortung der Theologie*, ed. Hans-Dieter Mutschler [Freiburg im Breisgau: Herder, 2001], 238). There are other lower case references in the English when Rahner refers to the idea of a "hypostatic union" in general. It appears the translator has simply used the context to distinguish these uses from the specific reference to the hypostatic union as it occurs in Christ.

spiritual subjects are not *hypostatically* united to the Logos in the narrow sense of "hypostatic union." When the Son of God takes to himself a human nature, he not only is united to an individual human nature, but also to humanity in a general sense. This assumption of a human nature is then the means by which union with humanity occurs:

> This "assumption" and "unification" has the nature of a self-communication; there is "assumption" so that God's reality may be communicated to what is assumed, viz. the human nature (and in the first place the human nature of Christ). But this very communication which is aimed at by this "assumption" is *the* communication by what we call grace and glory— and the latter are intended for all.[19]

For Rahner, God's self-communication occurs precisely *through* the assumption of human nature. It is the means by which divine self-communication happens—initially in Christ's specific human nature and subsequently for all people as Christ assumes human nature generally. He continues:

> But this very communication which is aimed at by this "assumption" is *the* communication by what we call grace and glory—and the latter are intended for all. It must not be objected that *this* (latter) communication is possible even without a hypostatic union, since it does in fact occur without it in our own case. For in us this communication is possible and effected precisely by this union and acceptance as it occurs in the Hypostatic Union. And, theologically speaking at least, there is nothing against the assumption that grace and hypostatic union can only be thought of together and that, as

19. Rahner, "Christology within an Evolutionary View of the World," 182.

a unity, they signify one and the same *free* decision of God to institute the supernatural order of salvation.[20]

Hypostatic union in the narrow sense makes possible hypostatic union in the broad sense. The gift of God's self-communication must always be wrapped in the union of divine and human natures, "for in us this communication is possible and effected precisely by this union and acceptance as it occurs in the Hypostatic Union."[21] He continues: "Hence, if we may put it this way, the Hypostatic Union does not differ from our grace by what is pledged in it, for this is grace in both cases (even in the case of Jesus). But it differs from our grace by the fact that Jesus is our pledge, and we ourselves are not the pledge but the recipients of God's pledge to us."[22]

The similarity between Christ's hypostatic union and our own lies in the grace that is given: communion with God himself. Christ in his human nature does not receive a different grace than the rest of humanity. The grace is the same, but for Christ, the grace is original. The uniqueness of Christ's hypostatic union lies particularly in the presence of the person of the Logos when the gift of grace is given to Christ's specific human nature. For Christ, pledge and recipient are identical; the union is an *auto*-union. In individual "hypostatic unions," the uncreated grace is not united to the one who offers, but to those who are strictly recipients.[23]

---

20. Ibid., 182.

21. Ibid.

22. Ibid., 183. By "grace" Rahner is referring to "uncreated grace," that is, God's gift of himself.

23. Ibid.

Conclusion

Rahner viewed Chalcedon as a beginning point. He was willing to allow his metaphysic to reinterpret Chalcedon, and he drastically reconceived theology for a contemporary context. He was able to situate the hypostatic union within God's grand plan of self-communication, specifically, an *ontological* self-communication that changes human *being*.

5

THE HYPOSTATIC
UNION AND DIVINE
SELF-COMMUNICATION

Having seen that Rahner treated the Chalcedonian formula as the beginning of a theological journey, we may now turn our attention to his destination. Rahner's metaphysical concerns led him to develop the hypostatic union in such a way that allowed for transformative effects in humans. This is God's climactic self-communication to humanity, accomplished through the incarnate Logos. All of humanity is represented in him, because he is, first, the possibility of transcendence and reception of God's self-communication and, second, the consummate acceptance of this gift of self in his own personal and existential experience. Jesus Christ became the absolute "yes" to the offer of divine grace (the climactic fundamental option), and, therefore, the hypostatic union is the fulcrum on which God's gracious plan for humanity is leveraged. In Jesus Christ, God does not merely provide a bridge between himself and the intended finite recipients of grace, but provides the metaphysical apex of this communication. In short, Jesus Christ actualizes the gift and reception of uncreated grace.

In order to understand how this may occur within Rahner's metaphysical and theological formulations, we must study more closely his understanding of the person of the Son, namely, whether and to what extent the person of the Son preexisted creation. We will then turn to Rahner's theology of the symbol, which explains the ontological character of God's transformative gift of himself to spirits in the world.

The Bridge between Eternity and History

The Preexistence of the Son

It may seem out of place to treat the preexistence of the Son at this juncture. Within a traditional *loci* approach, this subject would fall under the heading of the Trinity, which is chapter 2 of the present study. However, Rahner's unique approach to theology suggests we explore the eternal existence of the Son in conjunction with his concrete experience as human being, because the latter expresses the former. While Rahner does not use the specific terminology, the concepts of the *Logos ensarkos* (the incarnate Son) and the *Logos asarkos* (the preexistent Son without flesh) are clearly present in his theology. This may come as a surprise to those who give a strict realist interpretation to Rahner's Trinitarian axiom.[1] For Rahner, the Son's economy

---

1. Randal Rauser identifies three readings of Rahner's Trinitarian axiom: strict realist, loose realist, and strict antirealist. The strict realist reading identifies the immanent Trinity with the economic Trinity ontologically and exhaustively. The loose realist reading understands Rahner's axiom as an epistemological principle pertaining to how we come to know that God is one in three. Finally, the strict antirealist reading challenges whether truth claims about the Trinity are viable in a realist sense. Rather, they may be true according to pragmatism or coherentism. Rauser argues that each of the readings leaves the axiom either trivial or obviously false. See Randal Rauser,

refers first to his eternal procession from the Father and only then to his incarnation. While the Son preexists creation, his eternal relationship to the Father means that aspects of his "economy" precede creation as well. This is a significant difference from a confessionally Reformed understanding of economy, which arises from God's relation to creation. According to Rahner, the two may be distinguished in terms of their historical expression, yet there is an identity between the immanent Trinity and the economic Trinity and between the *Logos ensarkos* and the *Logos asarkos*. This allows Rahner to develop the deep congruence between God (the self-communicating revealer) and man (the divinely endowed recipient).

Man is not the pattern to which the Son must conform. Neither is the communication tailored to the hearer. The hearer is created specifically to receive this message. The Son does not come to be as an economic reality in history. The message is characterized from eternity as Logos-procession. The Father and Son relate to one another in this manner from eternity, and therefore their economic relation is not a new relation, but only a new expression of the previously existing eternal relation.[2] This is perhaps the most creative feature of Rahner's Trinitarian doctrine and one that many interpreters miss. The incarnation is not an entirely new reality for the Logos, because the hypostatic union is not so much an assumption of a human nature as it is a concrete historical expression of an eternal reality. Rahner says, "The question is this: is the humanity of the Logos merely something foreign which has been assumed, or is it precisely that which comes into being when the Logos ex-presses himself

---

"Rahner's Rule: An Emperor without Clothes?" *International Journal of Systematic Theology* 7, no. 1 (January 1, 2005): 81–94. Scott D. Harrower uses Rauser's categories in *Trinitarian Self and Salvation: An Evangelical Engagement with Rahner's Rule* (Eugene, OR: Pickwick Publications, 2012).

2. Karl Rahner, *The Trinity* (New York: Crossroad, 1997), 63n17.

into the non-divine?"[3] When the *ad intra* self-communication of the Father as the eternally begotten Son is expressed *ad extra* in history, it is expressed as the hypostatic union:[4] "Now Christ's 'human nature' is not something which happens to be there, among many other things, which might equally well have been hypostatically assumed, but it is precisely that which comes into being when God's Logos 'utters' himself outwards."[5] In other words, when the immanent relationship between Father and Son is demonstrated concretely, the Son becomes incarnate.

There is then a strong unity and even identity between the immanent and the economic Trinity, because they are eternal and concrete expressions, respectively, of the same being. Nonetheless, a proper order obtains between them. The Son's eternal procession as *ad intra* self-expression of the Father becomes the condition of possibility for the *ad extra* concrete-historical expression of that eternal reality. The Father's self-communication of the Son is "economic," yet "pre-exists."[6]

Rahner believed that his understanding of the hypostatic

---

3. Ibid., 31n27. Rahner argues that human history, by virtue of the hypostatic union, is God's history of self-expression: "This human history, by the very fact of being God's own pure and radical revelation, is the most living of all, the most free before God from the world towards God, and thus mediatorial, because it is the history of God himself *and* because it is supremely creaturely and free" (Karl Rahner, "Current Problems in Christology," in *Theological Investigations*, vol. 1, 2nd. ed., trans. Cornelius Ernst [Baltimore: Helicon, 1965], 163).

4. "We could now define man, within the framework of his supreme and darkest mystery, as that which ensues when God's self-utterance, his Word, is given out lovingly into the void of god-less nothing" (Karl Rahner, "On the Theology of the Incarnation," in *Theological Investigations*, vol. 4, trans. Kevin Smyth [Baltimore: Helicon, 1966], 116). "And the humanity of Christ is not the form in which God appears, in the sense of a vaporous and empty apparition which has no validity of its own in comparison with and in contrast to what is manifested. Since *God* himself 'goes out of' himself, this form of his existence has the most radical validity, force and reality" (Rahner, "On the Theology of the Incarnation," 117).

5. Rahner, *The Trinity*, 89.

6. Ibid., 64.

union was necessary to protect against Docetism, Apollinarism, monophysitism, monothelitism, and other heresies that compromise the integrity of Christ's human nature.[7] The human nature is necessary, real, and distinct from the divine nature, though native to it. It is not "foreign" in the sense that it is not proper to his eternal divine nature. It is the concrete-historical extension and expression of his eternal begottenness, the Father's self-communication. This is precisely the reason why Rahner was intent on affirming that only the Son could become incarnate.[8] The Father and the Holy Spirit could not be expressed as hypostatic union, because neither is eternally begotten. Being the only member of the Godhead with this distinguishing personal property, the Son is likewise the only hypostasis able to be communicated concretely to the world. This structure allows Rahner to connect the immanent and the economic Trinity while also leaving creation, revelation, and elevating grace contingent upon God's own free decision. The difference, then, between the immanent and the economic Trinity is not ontic, but modal-expressive.[9]

God works outside of himself generally and indiscriminately in creation (Ps. 19:1; Rom. 1:20). To use the language of the Westminster Standards, God is known through his works of creation and providence. In this way, the entire Godhead is revealed and known. Rahner distinguishes that type of *ad extra* work from self-communication, which in turn sets Rahner's formulation against Augustine's maxim that *all* of God's works *ad extra* are indivisible. In divine self-communication, the persons of the Godhead are revealed and known individually. In

---

7. Rahner, "On the Theology of the Incarnation," 118.

8. "There has occurred in salvation history something which can be predicated only of one divine person" (Rahner, *The Trinity*, 23).

9. This is a mode of expression, but since the eternal relation between the Father and Son always exists, Rahner's position does not resort to modalism.

other words, through divine self-communication, we come to know a specific person of the Trinity, not an undifferentiated Godhead. To accomplish this, Rahner establishes a new form of *ad extra* relation by linking an individual act *ad extra* with the native modal-expression of another nature. In other words, the economic identity and specific person of the Son come to be revealed and known through an assumed nature. A hypostatic union is necessary for any individual hypostasis to relate to the world individually, that is, without the other hypostases being involved as they are in all other acts *ad extra*: "For only in such a union is there actualized what is proper to the person, the personality, the 'outward' hypostatic function."[10] And what is proper to the Son is precisely what human beings can receive concretely in the world.

A Historical Window into the Trinity

When we study divine self-communication through the hypostatic union, we see aspects of the eternal person of the Son. The person unites the two natures, so that when we experience the person in history, we see the eternal one.[11] We may treat the hypostatic union as a means to access eternity through history. And because of this union, the person of the Son encounters himself through his existential human nature reaching out toward and receiving his own self as grace in his divine nature. Likewise, we encounter God as grace when we reach out.

Rahner believes that men are created as beings that "become" through a process of self-realization. They are existential beings that always question their existence in the world. They are also equipped with a range of universal human properties—existentials—that allow them to navigate that existence. As we

10. Ibid., 25.
11. Ibid., 62.

discussed earlier, one of those properties is the supernatural exis-tential, an inclination toward the divine mystery.

In hypostatic union, God may now experience himself and come to self-realization.[12] From eternity, God is pure act. But in hypostatic union, the Son of God has a special potency, allowing him to realize and transcend human experience. God can meet himself by experiencing the Trinitarian being through eminence, return, and self-realization. Man is distinguished from other types of created beings as one that is present to self, and the hypostatic union takes this general ontological reality to new heights. In the person of the incarnate Son, the eternal God encounters himself through the free acceptance of the free offer of uncreated grace.[13] God is able to become historically present to himself through the existential human experience of the Son of God. Both God and man can experience themselves and each other in a manner that is impossible, apart from their mutual relationship.[14]

Realsymbol

For Rahner, the relationship between God and man is revealed most clearly in the incarnation. The incarnation does not merely signify the relationship between God and man, but con-summates and develops the relationship according to Rahner's theology of the "symbol." The Logos revealed in history is the concrete expression or "exteriorization" of the eternal Logos.[15]

---

12. Rahner, "On the Theology of the Incarnation," 110.

13. "If man is thus the self-transcendence of living matter, then the history of nature and of spirit form an intrinsic and stratified unity in which the history of nature develops towards man, continues on in him as *his* history, is preserved and surpassed in him, and therefore reaches its own goal with and in the history of man's spirit" (Karl Rahner, *Foundations of Christian Faith: An Introduction to the Idea of Christianity* [New York: Seabury, 1978], 187).

14. By fashioning the divine-human relationship in this way, Rahner creatively develops the *exitus-reditus* scheme described in Thomas Aquinas's metaphysic.

15. "Man is possible because the exteriorization of the Logos is possible. . . . What Jesus is and does as man reveals the Logos himself; it is the reality of the Logos as our

The incarnate Son is the same communication from the Father as he is in eternity, though when this communication is expressed concretely, it occurs incarnationally through hypostatic union. The other side of that self-communication is man's existential inclination, by which he reaches out toward something greater than himself. God's revelation in history is not simply an appearance, but an ontic representation of his relationship with mankind: "If God wishes to step freely outside of himself, he must create man. There is no need to explain in detail that he must then create a spiritual-personal being, the only one who possesses the 'obediential potency' for the reception of such a self-communication."[16]

In order to respect divine and human freedom, while also guaranteeing that this self-communication will be given *and* received, the Son *must* become incarnate, uniting the free divine offer with a radically free human acceptance of that offer. Only in the incarnation does this self-communication find "its peak and irreversible finality."[17] God's gift of himself becomes definitive and irrevocable.[18] When the incarnation occurs, it forever stamps history with the finality of this personal relationship between God and man. Rahner's conception of a symbol transcends the concept of a basic signifier that merely points to or anticipates its referent. For Rahner, a *Realsymbol* not only denotes its referent, but also alters it. Consider the way in which an embrace might dynamically symbolize a marriage. The embrace not only

---

salvation amidst us. Then we can assert, in the full meaning of the words: here the Logos with God and the Logos with us, the immanent and the economic Logos, are strictly the same" (Rahner, *The Trinity*, 33).

16. Ibid., 89–90.

17. Ibid., 90.

18. If this offer of self-communication is a real and genuine offer to historic men, it must occur "definitively and irrevocably only when it is historically *there* in the 'absolute bringer of salvation,' when the proffering of divine self-communication not only constitutes a world as the addressee of its offer, but posits itself irrevocably as historical" (ibid., 95).

outwardly symbolizes the love between a husband and wife, but also intensifies it.[19] Likewise, Jesus Christ, the God-man, is the *Realsymbol* of God's love for mankind, embodying and intensifying that relationship in hypostatic union. Jesus Christ acts as the fulcrum for all of Rahner's theological anthropology. He is the climactic point of self-communication between God and man.

The Necessity of the Hypostatic Union

Rahner sought to fit his Christology "into the framework of an evolutionary world-view of a cosmos which evolves towards that spirit who attains absolute self-transcendence and perfection through and in an absolute self-communication given by God in grace and glory."[20] One noteworthy implication of this is the fact that for Rahner the incarnation has significance for humanity beyond redemption from sin. It is metaphysically and theologically necessary, independent of soteriology. In conjunction with several other Catholic theologians of his era, Rahner felt that modern Christologies underemphasize Christ's humanity and its role in bringing humans into the Trinitarian life.[21] As a result, much of Rahner's Christological writing tends to remedy the perceived problem. Although he did not regularly teach a course on Christology, his reflections on the human nature of Christ became a hallmark of his theological anthropology—and, to some extent, his entire theological program.

As we detailed in the preceding chapter, the hypostatic union functions as an archetype for all people. At the level of individual

19. James C. Livingston et al., *Modern Christian Thought: The Twentieth Century*, 2nd ed. (Minneapolis: Fortress, 2006), 212.

20. Karl Rahner, "Christology within an Evolutionary View of the World," in *Theological Investigations*, vol. 5, trans. Karl-H. Kruger (Baltimore: Helicon, 1966), 184.

21. Karl Adam, *The Christ of Faith: The Christology of the Church* (London: Burns & Oates, 1957).

human nature, the hypostatic union is repeated for each person when they receive God's personal offer of self-communication. Rahner draws this dimension of his Christology out as he broadens the typical understanding and referent of "hypostatic union." He suggests an analogy between Christ's hypostatic union and the salvation histories of individual people. The hypostatic union of the incarnate Son should be considered an archetype with referent ectypes instead of a master copy with clones. Because Christ has encountered himself through the incarnation, we now may also encounter God as gracious gift: "For in us this communication is possible and effected precisely by this union and acceptance as it occurs in the Hypostatic Union."[22] The difference between the archetype and its subsequent ectypes is not simply a matter of chronological order or the nature of what is given and received. The difference lies in the origin and recipient of the gift. The hypostatic union is "the absolute guarantee that this ultimate and basically unsurpassable self-transcendence will succeed and indeed has already begun."[23] Christ, as God-man, is the archetype of self-transcendence upon which Rahner can ground his theological anthropology. "Seen from this viewpoint, the Incarnation appears as the necessary and permanent beginning of the divinization of the world as a whole."[24]

The Jesuit Rahner adopts a Franciscan position, rather than follow the Dominicans, with whom the Jesuits have historically identified on this issue. The Franciscans follow Duns Scotus, who argues that the Son of God would have become incarnate even had sin not entered the world.[25] This complements

22. Rahner, "Christology within an Evolutionary View of the World," 182.
23. Ibid., 159.
24. Ibid., 159–60.
25. "It is therefore impossible to say that the view of the Incarnation proposed by us could arouse some real misgivings on the part of the *magisterium*. In the Catholic Church it is freely permitted to see the Incarnation first of all, in God's primary intention, as the summit and height of the divine plan of creation, and not primarily and

Rahner's desire for history to move toward a climactic divine self-communication, since the incarnation would have occurred even if Adam had not fallen into sin. Regardless of the outcome of Adam's probation, elevating grace would have been given so that humanity could enjoy the beatific vision. Rahner sees this happening specifically through the hypostatic union, which is not simply an event that allows for humanity to be redeemed. Independent of sin, it allows for humanity to transcend. History is moving toward a climactic synthesis in which God and man converge.[26] The human nature of Christ, then, is the vehicle through which God accomplishes his communicative and existential will, specifically and climactically in the person of Christ and then generally in human beings when they experience closeness to and immediacy with God.

The hypostatic union is not exclusively a redemptive event. It neither restores man to his original created estate nor reclaims an original offer of salvation. Rather, it is the beginning of an end in itself. Rahner's motivation for espousing the Scotist view becomes apparent in his understanding of grace.[27] As mentioned above, Rahner advocates an eschatology in which Adam would have enjoyed the immediate vision of God, had he not fallen into sin. Even in the prelapsarian order, a higher

---

in the first place as the act of a mere restoration of a divine world-order destroyed by the sins of mankind, an order which God had conceived in itself without any Incarnation" (ibid., 185).

26. "This antecedent self-communication of God which is prior to man's freedom means nothing else but that the spirit's transcendental movement in knowledge and love towards the absolute mystery is borne by God himself in his self-communication in such a way that this movement has its term and its source not in the holy mystery as eternally distant and as a goal which can only be reached asymptotically, but rather in the God of absolute closeness and immediacy" (Rahner, *Foundations of Christian Faith*, 129).

27. "Therefore this self-communication of God to spiritual creatures can and must be called supernatural and gratuitous even prior to sin, without thereby introducing into man's single reality a multi-leveled dualism" (ibid., 124).

mode of existence—the beatific vision—awaited mankind. God enabled man to reach out for this vision transcendentally, and he guaranteed the acceptance of this offer through the hypostatic union. Because the hypostatic union is a prelapsarian means for achieving this future, the categories of sin and redemption are minimized.

Interestingly, in the seminal work "Christology within an Evolutionary View of the World,"[28] the topics of sin and redemption are not mentioned until the very end. The entire discussion of hypostatic union in Christ, as well as in individuals (as analogues), occurs outside the context of redemption from sin. The hypostatic union is fundamentally a metaphysical necessity that transcends soteriology. But this does not mean it has no bearing upon sin.[29] For Rahner, forgiveness of sin happens when the sinner gives himself over to the mystery of God, and in doing so, ceases to be self-centered and self-sufficient. His description of guilt lacks the forensic dimension so prominent in Reformed and Lutheran formulations.[30] Forgiveness of sin comes through God's self-communication, because man's separation from God

28. Rahner, "Christology within an Evolutionary View of the World."

29. "It is the person who in the forlornness of his guilt still turns in trust to the mystery of his existence which is quietly present, and surrenders himself as one who even in his guilt no longer wants to understand himself in a self-centered and self-sufficient way, it is this person who experiences himself as one who does not forgive himself, but who is forgiven, and he experiences this forgiveness which he receives as the hidden, forgiving and liberating love of God himself, who forgives *in that* he gives himself, because only in this way can there really be forgiveness once and for all" (Rahner, *Foundations of Christian Faith*, 131).

30. "If we further inquire how this reconciliation through forgiveness of inherently insuperable guilt is to be conceived, we must first point out that Catholic theology must not conceive this forgiveness as a juridical act, an act that is more or less merely intellectual, upon which there merely follows the communication of divine grace, which is justification. Rather, this forgiveness takes place *through* divine grace, God's very communication of himself" (Karl Rahner, "Reconciliation and Vicarious Representation," in *Theological Investigations*, vol. 21, trans. Hugh M. Riley [London: Darton, Longman & Todd, 1988], 261).

is an ontological problem remedied by an ontological communication of God to man. God's ontological self-communication
provides forgiveness and justification without requiring a judi-
cial reckoning.[31] God's ontological self-communication brings
human beings into closer fellowship with him and therefore triumphs over any shortcomings in their lives. Through the gifts of
uncreated and elevating grace, human beings come to share in
the divine life.

The Personal and Transformative
Character of Self-Communication

We have been laboring to develop the Rahnerian thesis that
salvation is an ontological communication of the Trinitarian
self. The gift is personal because it proceeds from the divine will
and involves self-consciousness and freedom. Moreover, since
self-communication is indeed *self*-communication, the gift of
uncreated grace further establishes and transforms the personal
relationship between gift and giver. The ultimate gain in the gospel is not a benefit or thing, but a transformative relationship to a
person: "The term 'self-communication' is really intended to signify that God in his own most proper reality makes himself the
inner-most constitutive element of man. We are dealing, then,
with an *ontological* self-communication of God."[32] Rahner details
God's activity in forming a relationship with humanity, rather
than simply sending a message. He invites people to transcend

31. "Now the Christian message says in the doctrine of the so-called 'grace of
justification,' and especially in the doctrine of man's fulfillment in the vision of God,
that man is the event of an absolute and forgiving *self*-communication of God. 'Self-
communication' is meant here in a strictly ontological sense corresponding to man's
essential being, man whose being is being-present-to-himself, and being personally
responsible for himself in self-consciousness and freedom" (Rahner, *Foundations of
Christian Faith*, 117).

32. Ibid., 116.

themselves and at the same time enables them to respond to his invitation, thereby becoming a higher form of life. To describe this relation, Rahner uses Scholastic language.[33] God becomes a formal cause and the constitutive element in the creature's life. By communicating the divine life, God raises the creature to a higher, more fulfilled and immediate mode of existence.[34] This no doubt raises questions about the Creator-creature distinction. How can God give the gift of himself, or divine life, without making the creature god?[35] Rahner insists that when God communicates himself, he changes the recipients of his gracious gift without compromising his divine transcendence or distinction from creation:

> It is decisive for an understanding of God's self-communication to man to grasp that the giver in his own being is the gift, that in and through his own being the giver gives himself to creatures as their own fulfillment. Of course this divine self-

33. "In this mode of conceptualization it can then be said that in this self-communication God in his absolute being is related to the created existent in the mode of formal causality, that is, that he does not originally cause and produce something different from himself in the creature, but rather that he communicates his own divine reality and makes it a constitutive element in the fulfillment of the creature" (ibid., 121).

34. Mark F. Fischer notes that through ontological participation, God is immediately present in the gift and is shared with the creature (*The Foundations of Karl Rahner: A Paraphrase of the Foundations of Christian Faith, with Introduction and Indices* [New York: Crossroad, 2005], 41).

35. Rahner, *Foundations of Christian Faith*, 125. The Creator-creature distinction must be maintained, even in the hypostatic union. "If in the Incarnation the Logos enters into relationship with a creature, then it is obvious that the ultimate formal determinations of the Creator-creature relationship must also hold in *this* particular relationship. Hence the question remains entirely open as to whether the special character of the Incarnation, in so far as it is *distinguished* from all other relationships of God to a created thing, may be derived as a special case of this general property or not. A negative reply may be given to this question without its necessarily following that what we have said would have to be or could be contested" (Rahner, "Current Problems in Christology," 163).

communication, in which God makes himself a constitutive principle of the created existent without thereby losing his absolute, ontological independence, has "divinizing" effects in the finite existent in whom this self-communication takes place. As determinations of the finite existent itself, these effects must be understood as finite and created. But the real thing about this divine self-communication is the relationship between God and a finite existent, and this can and must be understood as analogous to a causality in which the "cause" becomes an intrinsic, constitutive principle of the effect itself.[36]

Determining precisely what Rahner means by "divinization" is difficult. He uses the term with reference to an ontological change—an elevation of existence.[37] Elsewhere he uses it as a synonym for sanctification.[38] And on occasion Rahner even

36. Rahner, *Foundations of Christian Faith*, 120. Also, "Divine self-communication means, then, that God can communicate himself in his own reality to what is not divine without ceasing to be infinite reality and absolute mystery, and without man ceasing to be a finite existent different from God" (ibid., 119).

37. Rahner says, for example, "The ontological nature of the doctrine of the immediate vision of God can be grasped in all its radicality only if it is understood as the natural fulfillment of that innermost and really *ontological divinization* of man which comes to expression in the doctrine of the justifying sanctification of man through the communication of the Holy Spirit to him. What grace and vision of God mean are two phases of one and the same event which are conditioned by man's free historicity and temporality. They are two phases of God's single self-communication to man" (ibid., 118 [emphasis added]).

38. For instance, Rahner says, "The words 'in itself' should be noted. All Catholic theologians are familiar with the view that the hypostatic union of the humanity of Christ with the Logos has as a necessary consequence the *intrinsic* divinization of this human nature. Though it is a consequence of the hypostatic union which is morally and indeed ontologically necessary, it is distinct from the union, and through it alone is the humanity of Christ sanctified and divinized 'in itself'—and (though in a unique measure of intrinsic holiness) is precisely that which is to be bestowed on all men as grace of justification" (Rahner, "On the Theology of the Incarnation," 112n2). Rahner also speaks of being divinized by the Spirit in prayer. See Karl Rahner, "Some Theses on Prayer," in *Theological Investigations*, vol. 5, trans. Karl-H. Kruger (Baltimore: Helicon, 1966), 422–23.

refers to divinization—in conjunction with union with Christ—in terms of justification.[39]

For Rahner, "the Incarnation appears as the necessary and permanent beginning of the divinization of the world as a whole."[40] In the incarnation and hypostatic union, there is both a *Realsymbol* and a guarantee of an elevated existence for humanity. Considered more closely, divinization through self-communication is God making himself the constitutive principle of the recipient, and this is analogous to the Scholastic language of formal causality. The gift of uncreated grace leads to a created effect that Rahner describes as an inner quality of transformation.[41] Hence, Christ comes to be the *Realsymbol* of God's self-communication to humanity. Not only does he symbolize the divine self-communication of God to man in that

---

39. "Man's divinization by the created and uncreated grace of Christ at the same time—and in equal proportion and measure—brings about a union with Christ as the Head of his Mystical Body which is the Church. The sharing in the divine nature and the union with Christ are simply two inseparable aspects of the same process of justification" (Rahner, "Some Theses on Prayer," 424). The hypostatic union is the absolute guarantee that this self-communication and subsequent divinization will occur. It is the alpha-point of a "final phase" and "final climax" in which man is united to "the absolute mystery called God" (Rahner, "Christology within an Evolutionary View of the World," 160–61).

40. Rahner, "Christology within an Evolutionary View of the World," 160–61.

41. He writes, "Being led by the Spirit (Rom. 8:14), glowing with the Spirit (Rom. 12:11), being sanctified and justified in the Spirit (1 Cor. 2:15; 6:11), being made to drink of the Spirit, anointed and sealed by it, creation, renewal, rebirth, strengthening, illumination (by the Spirit, Christ, grace) (Eph. 3:16; Tim [*sic*] 1:12; 2 Tim 2:1; Eph. 1:18; 5:14; Heb. 6:4), etc., all these also essentially imply or embrace an inner transformation of the justified as such, hence an inner quality which inheres in him, hence what scholastic theology calls created grace. The same result may be derived from texts which speak in a partitive sense of the gift of the Spirit (Titus 3:5; Heb. 6:4) or of the earnest and the first-fruits of the Spirit (2 Cor. 1:22; 5:5; Rom. 8:23), using expressions, that is to say, in which the genitive ('of the Spirit') can doubtless be understood as not merely epexegetic but at least in a partitive sense as well" (Karl Rahner, "Some Implications of the Scholastic Concept of Uncreated Grace," in *Theological Investigations*, vol. 1, trans. Cornelius Ernst [Baltimore: Helicon, 1969], 321).

Christ *is* both God and man, but Christ also *becomes* the new humanity. He is constitutive of humanity, which is also part of that *Realsymbol.* The entire scope of salvation involves a transformation that is the result of uncreated grace:

> It is not difficult to see the basis of this conception: "uncreated grace" (God's communication of himself to man, the indwelling of the Spirit) implies a new *relation* of God to man. But this can only be conceived of as founded upon an absolute entitative modification of man himself, which modification is the real basis of the new real relation of man to God upon which rests the relation of God to man.[42]

This "entitative modification" becomes the basis of God's relation to man and vice versa. It is nothing less than a strongly ontological understanding of the beatific vision:

> This absolute entitative modification and determination of man is created grace, which has in consequence a twofold aspect: it is ontologically the formal basis of the analogical supernatural participation in God's nature through entitative assimilation of man to God's spirituality and holiness (*consortium formale*), and it is the basis of a special relation (union, indwelling) between man and God himself (*consortium terminativum*).[43]

God triumphs over sin through an ontological gift of the divine self, namely, the indwelling of the Holy Spirit as uncreated grace. God's eternal desire has been to communicate himself to humanity, transforming humans and raising them to an elevated

42. Ibid., 322.
43. Ibid., 322–23.

form of existence, and then to return to himself in concrete self-realization.[44]

Conclusion

For Rahner, the incarnation has ontological bearing upon those within its purview. Christ unites himself to humanity and becomes the *Realsymbol* of the divine self-communication to mankind. When the eternal Son of God expresses himself concretely, it is as a hypostatic union of divine and human natures, a union which guarantees the perfect union of divine self-gift and human acceptance of that gift in freedom. Christ is the new humanity, and the church is caught up with him as a continuation of that incarnation. For that reason, Christ's specific hypostatic union becomes an archetype for the ontological union that is repeated in each individual salvation history. Whenever individual human beings reach out toward the divine mystery and accept his free offer of self, there is ectypal hypostatic union, for what is received is a *person*, the *hypostasis* of the Holy Spirit. This personal gift of uncreated grace becomes constitutive of humanity, effecting an inward and *entitative* change. The personal gift of the divine self elevates the personal recipient of that gift.

---

44. Rahner references the work of Matthias Joseph Scheeben, who considers the entire scope of salvation as an overarching program of adoptive transformation. Scheeben's doctrine is conceived primarily, perhaps even exclusively, in terms of transformation. Scheeben describes the purpose of Adam's spiritual endowment: "It means, further, that God wills to be an adoptive Father to man, and as such wishes to be honored and glorified by man as by His adopted child. It means that God, not content with His natural relations to creatures and with those of creatures to Himself, wills to establish a far more intimate and tender relationship, from which a higher beatitude should arise for His creatures, and a wholly new glorification for Himself. And since all creation, both spiritual and corporal, is represented in man, God's supernatural, mysterious cosmic plan is centered in man, not in the angels" (Matthias Joseph Scheeben, *The Mysteries of Christianity* [St. Louis: B. Herder Book Co., 1947], 357).

It also elevates the giver. Through the hypostatic union, God is able to encounter himself in reflexive self-presence, actualizing a new form of personality even for him. This is the essence of Rahner's project: to explain the grounds of possibility and the requisite means for the triune gift of self. To evaluate whether he has succeeded, we will now turn to a series of extended criticisms.

6

A PROPOSAL FOR
PERICHORETIC PERSONALITY

Given our preceding discussion, the reader may recognize that Rahner's basic theological agenda is bound to a foundational question: how does God communicate himself to humanity? We have thus far labored to provide a faithful exposition of Rahner's theology by tracing the thread of this basic question throughout the theological disciplines. To paint an accurate portrait, we have taken care to reserve any significant criticisms until this point. We now turn to them.

Rahner helpfully identifies the unity between the love of God and the love of neighbor. In so doing, he also stresses the personal context in which human beings live. Man can never escape God. In fact, he always knows and experiences God. Formally, Rahner has much in common with Reformed theologians on these matters. Whereas Rahner develops the supernatural existential and the *Vorgriff auf esse,* Reformed theologians speak of the *sensus divinitatus.* Such formal similarity extends also to Rahner's insistence that salvation is about a personal relationship with God. This is admirable, especially considering that contemporary theologians run the risk of missing the proverbial forest for the trees. Reformed theologians in particular must beware of the danger of spending so much effort detailing the finer points of the *ordo salutis* to the neglect of the main point: that *all* of God's work on behalf of his people has been for the purpose of bringing them into closer union and communion with him to his glory. An elevated personal relationship transcends soteriology as the goal of human history. This adds context to the God-human relation by demonstrating that salvation is not concerned merely with receiving created benefits. The recipients of saving grace participate in the divine life—enjoying fellowship with Father, Son, and Holy Spirit. They are made like God by being transformed into his image and glory (Rom. 8:29; 2 Cor. 3:18; 1 John 3:2). While Rahner's emphasis on this eschatological and consummative relationship is warranted, his method for achieving it is open to a line or two of critique from a Reformed point of view.

Methodological Starting Point

Our criticism begins with methodology. Rahner's theological methodology becomes evident when he links the Trinity itself with salvation: "The isolation of the treatise of the Trinity *has* to be wrong. There *must* be a connection between Trinity and man. The Trinity is a mystery of *salvation*, otherwise it would never have been revealed."[1] Rahner identifies the Trinity as "a mystery of salvation" and immediately distinguishes his position from more traditional theologies that would identify the Trinity independent of any salvific consideration or, more generally speaking, creation. It would appear, therefore, that Rahner's method does not reflect the truth that God exists as the Trinity

---

1. Karl Rahner, *The Trinity* (New York: Crossroad, 1997), 21.

in himself, independent of any *ad extra* action. Instead, Rahner's theological method is anthropocentric.[2] To understand the significance of this approach, we must press further to see how it influences the development and use of his Trinitarian axiom.

Rahner's Trinitarian axiom is perhaps his single most influential contribution to contemporary theology. When readers first encounter his rule, they may be tempted to read Rahner as an unabashed modalist. In such a view, the Father, Son, and Spirit are merely various ways by which the one divine essence interacts with the world. If the world did not come to be, these ways of interacting with the world would be unnecessary. But, as we saw in chapter 5, Rahner's view is much more nuanced. He offers a sophisticated method for negotiating the immanent and economic aspects within his axiom. His explanation rests upon deep congruence between the distinguishable immanent and economic aspects of God's being, thus avoiding exhaustive identity. The hypostatic union is the concrete-historical manifestation of the Father's self-communication of the Son, which has occurred from eternity. The economic existence is substantially related to the immanent, but the economic neither constitutes nor exhausts the immanent. For Rahner to say that the immanent Trinity and the economic Trinity are the same is to say, first, that the two refer to the same God and, second, that the intra-Trinitarian economic relations revealed in history disclose eternal relations. For that reason, the economic *is* the immanent. The former does not introduce new intra-Trinitarian relationships, but only new expressions of the same eternal

---

2. Paul Molnar has criticized Rahner extensively for espousing a theological method that takes its departure from human experience. Molnar's analysis is helpful, but he fails to adequately connect the problems of Rahner's methodology to his doctrine of Trinitarian personality. See Paul Molnar, *Divine Freedom and the Doctrine of the Immanent Trinity: In Dialogue with Karl Barth and Contemporary Theology* (London/New York: T&T Clark, 2002), 83–124.

relationships. For example, Rahner affirms the preexistence of the Son of God; therefore, the Son cannot come into being as a response to anything in creation. He exists eternally independent of creation. However, tension arises within Rahner's theology, because his consideration of the Son always has in view the idea of self-communication. Rahner's theological methodology, which begins with human experience, has everything to do with this conclusion.

There is always an orientation toward a personal "other" within the Trinity. Because of Rahner's conception of intra-Trinitarian personality, this theological method compromises the doctrine of simplicity. For example, if God is absolutely independent and self-sufficient, he neither lacks nor needs any person or thing outside of himself. But in Rahner's Trinitarian formulation, he must move outside of the Trinity to find a genuine, personal "other" who may receive the Father's self-communication. But to speak of anything other than God as *absolute* or *essential* to God's existence is incoherent. In response, any consideration of simplicity or aseity must begin with the Trinity. The Trinity itself is absolute, self-contained, and self-referential, and it did not come to be. It is God's eternal being, and theological method should reflect this fact. If theological method presupposes something to the contrary, it cannot arrive at a correct doctrine of God.[3] Since Rahner's theological method begins with human experience and presupposes God's need to communicate himself to a genuine "other," human experience unwittingly becomes determinative of God's being.

3. James E. Dolezal defends the compatibility of simplicity and Trinity in light of Aquinas's metaphysics by demonstrating how real distinctions between the divine persons do not entail separation, division, or compartmentalization of the divine essence. Dolezal posits a real distinction among the divine persons, but not between each divine person and the divine substance. See James E. Dolezal, "Trinity, Simplicity and the Status of God's Personal Relations," *International Journal of Systematic Theology*, 2013, https://doi.org/10.1111/ijst.12016.

Although we inevitably theologize from within human experience, that experience is not foundational to God's being. Our doctrine of God must not, indeed cannot, *begin* with human experience. It must begin with God's independent existence. For that reason, theological method must be *indirect*. As finite creatures, human beings may not examine God's existence as a scientist studies the subjects of experimentation. Such a direct method precludes a proper doctrine of God from the start, because it presupposes the ability of human beings to access God through their own faculties. Even if we recognize those faculties as endowments from the Creator, the epistemological reference point in a direct approach is located in man. But the triune God is the self-authenticating, infinite, eternal Creator and sustainer of the world. Being finite, man depends upon the triune God at every point—including rational investigation and theologizing. A direct approach presupposes independence from such a God and therefore also precludes one from being discovered through such a method. Instead, theological methodology should begin with the triune God as its first principle and universal epistemological reference point. This God is transcendent and incomprehensible.

Nevertheless, it is possible to theologize about God's *in se* existence because he has revealed himself. If God had not revealed himself, humans would know nothing of his independent existence, let alone his intra-Trinitarian relations.[4] Granted, this revelation is less than exhaustive, but it is nonetheless true, and it forms a foundation for nonspeculative theology. Theological methodology must begin with the presupposition (or fundamental commitment) of the triune God as he has revealed himself in the Bible. God is fully able and willing to disclose truth about

---

4. This is only a manner of speaking hypothetically. Humans are themselves revelatory of God specifically as creatures made in his image.

his *a se* existence to human beings. It does not follow that all things are revealed for the purposes of salvation. Rahner himself rejects this idea implicitly through his formulations of protology and eschatology. For him, God's gift of grace would have existed even if man had never fallen into sin. In that scenario, the gift of uncreated grace cannot properly be a "mystery of salvation."[5] Yet, if Rahner insists that the Trinity itself is a mystery of salvation, he decouples uncreated grace, God's gift of *himself*, from the Trinity. How can we consider God's gift of himself outside of salvation when God's triune being is itself a mystery of salvation? Clearly, Rahner's theological method causes problems for his theology of self-communication.

Although Rahner does not presuppose the Trinity as his methodological starting point, he does challenge the traditional distinction expressed in Aquinas's treatises *De Deo uno* and *De Deo trino*: "The Bible and the Greeks would have us start from the one unoriginate God, who is already *Father* even when nothing is known as yet about generation and spiration. He is known as the one unoriginate hypostasis which is not *positively* conceived as 'absolute' even before it is explicitly known as relative."[6] Aquinas applies the nature-grace distinction to Trinitarian theology and epistemology. As humans contemplate creation through unaided reason, he argues, they can only conclude the unity of God. Only when God reveals himself in grace can humans learn that he exists as Trinity. This dualistic methodology suggests two gods: one known according to reason operating upon nature and another known by faith in terms of grace.

Favoring an Eastern-inspired Trinitarian theology, Rahner questions the distinction's usefulness. By beginning with the treatise on the one God, Rahner believes, theologians may only

5. Rahner, *The Trinity*, 21.
6. Ibid., 17.

make formal statements regarding the persons of the Trinity. He is only comfortable with the treatise on the unity of God so long as it is understood concretely. For him, God never exists merely in the abstract, and so Rahner moves further than Aquinas's distinction by linking the primacy of divine unity to revelation. Rahner admits that "although it is certainly incorrect to claim that this separation and sequence follow the course of revelation, which would also have progressed from a revelation of the divine essence to a revelation of the three persons, this separation and sequence may be considered more a didactic than a fundamental problem."[7] Regardless of whether this distinction is a "didactic" or "fundamental" problem, it has methodological significance. Even though he challenges Aquinas's distinction, he nevertheless presents another type of distinction when he indicates a shift from unity to diversity in God's revelation: "We might say at least with equal right that the history of revelation first reveals God as unoriginate person in his relation to the world, and next proceeds to the revelation of this person as the origin of intra-divine, personalizing vital processes."[8] In Rahner's assessment, traditional Western approaches to the Trinity begin with abstract metaphysical properties of God rather than the explicit experience of him "in salvation history in his free relations to his creatures."[9] He suggests that the Western approach fails because it considers God in the abstract. But while Rahner challenges the traditional approach and formal consideration, he simply moves them both into the sphere of the concrete-historical. The result accords with his axiom; revelation and the human experience of God in history are at the heart of his theological methodology.

Rahner's concrete revelational approach is no less problematic than Aquinas's traditional distinction. God does not exist

7. Ibid., 20.
8. Ibid., 20n15.
9. Ibid., 18.

in two ways, nor does he reveal himself in components. He is indivisibly triune, revealing himself truly, but not exhaustively. The one true God is always triune, and if he is known at all, he is known in that way. His invisible attributes have been "clearly perceived, ever since the creation of the world, in the things that have been made" (Rom. 1:20). If unaided reason leads one to conclude that God is one and at the same time does not conclude that he is triune, it concludes something that is less than divine. Divine unity is not the whole truth of the matter, and it must never be considered independently of divine diversity.

Gregory Nazianzus provides help with regard to these methodological concerns. He speaks of

> the infinite conjunction of Three Infinite Ones, Each God when considered in Himself; as the Father so the Son, as the Son so the Holy Ghost; the Three One God when contemplated together; Each God because Consubstantial; One God because of the Monarchia. No sooner do I conceive of the One than I am illumined by the Splendour of the Three; no sooner do I distinguish Them than I am carried back to the One. When I think of any One of the Three I think of Him as the Whole, and my eyes are filled, and the greater part of what I am thinking of escapes me. I cannot grasp the greatness of That One so as to attribute a greater greatness to the Rest. When I contemplate the Three together, I see but one torch, and cannot divide or measure out the Undivided Light.[10]

Gregory offers an approach that accounts for the finitude of human comprehension. The unity and diversity in the Godhead

---

10. Gregory Nazianzus, "Oration 40, The Oration on Holy Baptism," New Advent, accessed June 7, 2019, http://www.newadvent.org/fathers/310240.htm. John Calvin interacts with Gregory's statement in *Institutes of the Christian Religion*, 1.13.17.

are equally ultimate, and to contemplate one immediately draws us back to the other. Colin Gunton elaborates upon the methodological significance of Gregory's comments:

> If there are transcendentals, they will, as we have seen, be found in the dynamic interaction of the mind and that about which it thinks. The interesting point about Gregory is that that is precisely what we find: a dynamic dialectic between the oneness and the threeness of God of such a kind that the two are both given equal weight in the processes of thought. Thinking about God denies his mind rest in either unity or plurality, in Parmenides or Heraclitus.[11]

Gunton is right to point out the oscillation from oneness to threeness when contemplating the Trinity, though designating this oscillation "dialectic" is troublesome—at least if it is intended in a Hegelian sense of progress or movement toward some eschatological goal. This may lead to a misunderstanding of the human ability to comprehend the Trinity. We never overcome the oscillation of our thoughts from the one to the three and back again. While we maintain that we can know certain things about the Trinity, our thoughts never exhaust the Godhead, nor does a supposedly dialectic oscillation from oneness to threeness and back again move beyond this "Nazienzen Circle." At some point, we must be satisfied to rest in the mystery that an essentially triune God has revealed. But Rahner's method cannot do this, and his methodological faults run throughout his theology as an undercurrent drawing us to the following criticisms.

---

11. Colin E. Gunton, *The One, the Three, and the Many: God, Creation, and the Culture of Modernity: The 1992 Bampton Lectures* (Cambridge/New York: Cambridge University Press, 1993), 149–50.

Trinitarian Self-Consciousness

Intra-Trinitarian, Inter-Personal Relationships

Because Rahner's conception of personality involves freedom and agency, it is of utmost importance to consider his theology of Trinitarian self-consciousness. Self-consciousness is a necessary precondition for both freedom and agency: "The concept of *person* as the ontological principle of a free active centre, self-conscious, present to itself and through itself in being, is a concept which, in the sense just indicated, has always played round the edge of the most static and objective concept of *person*."[12] His emphasis on these aspects of personality becomes problematic once he identifies the Son as an eternal self-communication of the Father. Within Rahner's theology, self-communication is a thoroughly interpersonal activity, and for this type of exchange to occur, there must be a free giver and a free recipient. Thus, in order to characterize the Son as an eternal self-communication of the Father, we must identify the recipient of this self-communication. We might anticipate the recipient of the Father's eternal self-communication being either the Spirit or the Son himself, since both are eternal *hypostases*. But since Rahner affirms that God is uni-conscious to the exclusion of tri-conscious, he precludes any possibility of finding a genuinely personal other within the Trinity.

And so we are compelled to ascertain whether this conception of person applies to the unity of the Godhead, its diversity, or both. Early in his important book *The Trinity*, Rahner affirms that "God in general is a person."[13] This is important to Rahner, because God's personality forms the possibility and foundation of man's personality. Rahner identifies this ground specifically

12. Karl Rahner, "Current Problems in Christology," in *Theological Investigations*, vol. 1, 2nd ed., trans. Cornelius Ernst (Baltimore: Helicon, 1965), 159.

13. Rahner, *The Trinity*, 28.

with the unity (essence) of the Godhead.[14] Personality in the sense of free agency, self-awareness, and self-consciousness applies to God "in general," which is more closely related to his unity. Rahner then augments this essential self-consciousness with freedom, which for him is a basic category that undergirds the personal context in which self-communication occurs.

God communicates himself in grace freely, while at the same time humans receive the gift freely. If either party fails to express freedom, there may be no truly *personal* self-communication. Although Rahner presupposes freedom as a constitutive element of any gift of self, he is hesitant to make freedom constitutive of *hypostases*. This leads us to inquire in what sense the Son and Spirit are eternal self-communications. For example, the Father could not freely withhold the communications of the Son and Spirit, because the *hypostases* are necessary self-communications. Still, they do not possess self-consciousness or freedom absolutely, as the Father does. It appears that on Rahner's own terms, the *hypostases* cannot be *free* self-communications from the Father without making them subordinate to the divine essence and the Father. The Son and Spirit, as derivative self-communications,

---

14. "The ground of our spiritual personhood, which in the transcendental structure of our spiritual self always discloses itself as the ground of our person and at the same time remains concealed, has thereby revealed itself as person. The notion that the absolute ground of all reality is something like an unconscious and impersonal cosmic law, an unconscious and impersonal structure of things, a source which empties itself out without possessing itself, which gives rise to spirit and freedom without itself being spirit and freedom, the notion of a blind, primordial ground of the world which cannot look at us even if it wants to, all of this is a notion whose model is taken from the context of the impersonal world of things. It does not come from that source in which a basic and original transcendental experience is really rooted: namely, from a finite spirit's subjective and free experience of itself. In its very constitution a finite spirit always experiences itself as having its origins in another and as being given to itself from another—from another, therefore, which it cannot misinterpret as an impersonal principle" (Karl Rahner, *Foundations of Christian Faith: An Introduction to the Idea of Christianity* [New York: Seabury, 1978], 75.)

come into consideration as divine *persons* only with respect to the Father's personality and freedom.

The Personality of the Father

Rahner is convinced that if the traditional immanent-economic distinction held, it would compromise the possibility of a genuine gift of the divine self. If the economic Trinity is not identical to the immanent Trinity, the gift that is given could not be God; it would be a creature.[15] If the immanent Trinity is different from the economic, God would still exist transcendentally, but in Rahner's view he could not be known or received. He would remain wholly other and could only communicate a mediation of himself. For Rahner, this would compromise the truly interpersonal relationship of grace that God desires to establish with humanity.[16] God communicates himself immediately through the Son and Spirit.

Leaning upon the Eastern church, Rahner identifies the Father with the divine essence in a way that he does not do with the Son or the Spirit. In fact, according to Rahner, monotheism would be compromised if the diversity of *hypostases* were afforded equal ultimacy with the unity of essence. It is critical to maintain monotheism, but Rahner does so at the expense of the single greatest Christian distinctive, the Trinity. He seems to equate intra-Trinitarian plurality with quantity. From this basic premise, Rahner concludes that the unity of the Godhead must be primary, and it must be understood as personal singularity. Because Rahner does not begin with the Trinity as his methodological (and ontological) starting point, he comes to identify monotheism with the essence of God. He reasons that, since

15. Rahner, *The Trinity*, 100.
16. Karl Rahner, "Oneness and Threefoldness of God in Discussion with Islam," in *Theological Investigations*, vol. 18, trans. Edward Quinn (New York: Crossroad, 1983), 115.

monotheism is the belief in one God, and the unity of God is his essence, then the unity must be more basic to monotheism than the diversity of the Godhead.

It is apparent that Rahner's theological methodology, which begins with human experience, directs his conclusions. At the same time, a desire for ecumenicity is another significant influence. In his essay "Oneness and Threefoldness of God in Discussion with Islam," Rahner likens Christian monotheism to Islamic and Jewish monotheism.[17] By prioritizing unity over diversity, Rahner offers common ground to other religions, seeking rapprochement by making Christian ontological distinctives secondary. In so doing, Rahner surrenders the very distinctiveness of Christian ontology, inevitably prioritizing the unity of the essence over the diversity of the *hypostases*.[18] Although Rahner rejects the idea of an abstract absolute oneness behind the God of history, his formulations result in one.[19]

The Personal Status of the Son and Spirit

Since the Father is the unoriginate God who nevertheless communicates himself in two factualities,[20] it seems that Rahner

17. Ibid., 121.

18. In his essay on the Trinity and Islam, Rahner minimizes the language of diversity within the Godhead, opting for a conclusion that sees Christian and Islamic monotheism as basically identical or at least compatible. Having conceded this point, thus giving up the most basic Christian distinctive, Rahner is in a position to question whether the Christian notion of diversity within the Godhead should be a significant issue for Muslims: "As I said at the very beginning, I am aware that I have not really carried out a dialogue with Islamic theology, but only indicated a few points from the problems within Christianity with reference to monotheism and the doctrine of the Trinity, in the modest hope that it might perhaps be remotely useful for a real dialogue in which Islamic and Christian theologians would talk about a joint profession of faith in the one sole God and ask at the same time why this profession is not curtailed or threatened by the Christian doctrine of the threefoldness of this one sole God" (ibid., 121).

19. Ibid., 107.

20. Rahner, *The Trinity*, 84; Rahner, *Foundations of Christian Faith*, 118.

must necessarily grant priority to the Father. Whether this priority is only with reference to person or is also ontological, or something else, remains to be seen. As we noted, Rahner rejects the idea that those modes of factuality are created forms of mediation between God and his creatures, because God's self-communication is a genuine communication of himself, not a created reality. Furthermore, Rahner insists that the economic relations must be identical with the immanent relations, or else we resort to economic Sabellianism and Arianism.[21] These personal ontological guidelines direct Rahner's development of Christ's personality. As self-communications originating from the Father, the *hypostases*-factualities necessarily presuppose a personal object as the free recipient of their mode of existence. But to this point we still have not identified any genuinely personal recipient. In search of one, we must further explore the personal status of the Son and Spirit within Rahner's theology.

Rahner affirmed the orthodox formula that Christ is one person and two natures, but since he also distinguished between creedal and philosophical senses of the word "person," he may augment the orthodox formula:

> And it immediately follows once again that the purely *formal* (abstract) schema *nature-person* is inadequate. We must conceive of the relation between the Logos-Person and his human nature in just this sense, that here *both* independence *and* radical proximity equally reach a unique and qualitatively incommensurable perfection, which nevertheless remains once and for all the perfection of a relation between Creator and creature. But in view of the fact that this simultaneous perfection can only be realized in a creature with regard to *God*, it becomes even clearer that the abstract concept of a "person who has a nature"

---

21. Rahner, *The Trinity*, 38.

is not enough to allow us to infer this characteristic feature of Christ's human liberty with respect to God, a feature which is of such decisive significance for him and which characterizes him as Man and Mediator. This liberty is possible only when the person who has this free nature is either identical with this nature or is the *divine* Person as divine. And in this way it becomes clear how necessary it is to go beyond this "Two-natures-one-Person" formula.[22]

If (1) self-consciousness and self-awareness are distinguishing characteristics of personality and (2) God is strictly uni-conscious, then (3) the Son's distinctive personality, which is associated with his self-consciousness and self-awareness, must be exclusively human. This is highly problematic, for according to this formulation, the Son lacks *in se* divine personality proper to himself. Indeed, the use of "himself" is a category error. Such a view compromises any personal awareness the Son may possess regarding his status as eternally begotten of the Father, any reciprocal relationships of love that he may have with the Father or Spirit, and any personal agency he might express in agreeing to save his people. Although these consequences of Rahner's view are regrettable in their own right, his development of the Spirit's eternal personality is even more wanting.

At times, Rahner places the Son and Spirit on equal footing as twin aspects of God's unified self-communication. The Son serves as the self-communication to the concrete-historical aspect of humanity, while the Spirit serves as the spirit-transcendent aspect. However, it becomes difficult for Rahner to maintain equal ultimacy between the Son and the Spirit once he turns to Christology. Rahner's development of the Son as *Realsymbol*

---

22. Rahner, "Current Problems in Christology," 162–63. In the philosophical sense involving free agency and self-consciousness, Christ is two persons (ibid.,158).

results in his prioritizing the Son over the Spirit. The Spirit has no preeminent symbolic manifestation, as does the Son. Instead, the Spirit is reduced to an aspect of Christ's personal experience—his transcendent reaching out toward the divine mystery—which is itself subjected to the Father's personality. It can be seen why Rahner finds great affinity with the Eastern tradition. By rejecting the *filioque* (the procession of the Spirit from *both* the Father and the Son), Eastern Trinitarian theology can subject the Son's personality to the Father and then the Spirit's personality to the Son.

The Primacy of Unity

The personality of the Father must be of a different order. The Son and Spirit derive their personality from the Father, and Rahner identifies the Father with the divine essence to the exclusion, or at least demotion, of the Son and Spirit. This eliminates any lasting possibility of equal ultimacy between the unity and diversity of the Godhead. By definition, there may be only one *absolute* personality. Since the Father's personality is of another order, the Father, Son, and Spirit cannot share equally in that absolute personality. At best, it will be original to one and derivative to the others.

This derivative personality comes to bear upon the possibility of an *ad intra* self-communication. If the *hypostases* exist concretely as self-communications, yet there is no substantial personal other, then there is also no genuinely interpersonal relation. For Rahner, "self-awareness is not a moment which distinguishes divine 'persons' one from another, even though each divine 'person' as concrete, possesses a self-consciousness."[23] While Rahner affirms that each *hypostasis* "possesses" a

---

23. Rahner, *The Trinity*, 75.

consciousness, he intends this in the sense that each *hypostasis* subsists in the divine essence. Still, this consciousness cannot distinguish the *hypostases* from one another. Scripture is clear that the Son is aware of his eternal distinction from the Father. He has always known that he in particular is the Son (John 17:5; Col. 1:15–20; Heb. 1:1–3). Likewise, the Spirit must know from eternity that he is distinct from the Father and the Son, even while they indwell one another exhaustively (1 Cor. 2:10–13). This is the great mystery of intra-Trinitarian relations; they express distinction without separation. With regard to personality and self-consciousness, the *hypostases* share exhaustively in uni-consciousness while also demonstrating personally distinct consciousness and eternal self-awareness. In terms of absolute personality with regard to self-consciousness, there is only one divine person for Rahner, and that is the Father. Again, he does not state explicitly that the Son and Spirit are created realities or divine manifestations that originated within *Heilsgeschichte*. He affirms that they are the preexistent conditions of possibility for God's self-communication to man. Nevertheless, on his own terms Rahner cannot account for their essential and absolute divine existence.

The unity and diversity of the Godhead are inextricably linked with the Father's self-communication. The Father is properly the person who communicates, as the unoriginate *hypostasis*. The Son and Spirit are two aspects of his unified, yet twofold, self-communication. Even though this self-communication is free, Rahner rejects the notion of an abstract entity behind the self-communication who could choose to withhold such a communication. And at times he argues that the Father himself is a "self-communication," though one of a different order.[24] But this

---

24. "For, on the one hand, it cannot be denied 'economically' that the Father himself gives himself in the Son and the Spirit, that he is thus 'immanently' himself insofar as he has Son and Spirit as the recipients of *his* essence; on the other hand,

does not seem to comport with Rahner's own characterization of self-communication. His theology cannot support an unequivocal notion of self-communication or of *hypostasis*. He must equivocate between senses whenever he refers to the unoriginate Father or the self-communicative Son and Spirit. And while it remains to be seen what is being communicated and to whom, Rahner did not believe that traditional Catholic theology fared any better:

> They [Son and Spirit] can no longer be really understood as the inner, mutually related moments of the one self-communication, through which God (the Father) communicates himself to the world unto absolute proximity. It follows that the difference between the incarnation and the descent of the Spirit, insofar as both of them are soteriological realities, is not clear.[25]

Neither Rahner nor traditional Catholic theology, as he understood it, can distinguish precisely between the Son and the Spirit. Lacking an appropriate doctrine of *perichoresis*, Rahner's theological problems multiply. A free self-communication presupposes self-awareness, consciousness, and agency. But Rahner insists that self-awareness is not a moment that distinguishes the *hypostases* from one another. Each *hypostasis* has *a* consciousness because each subsists in the essence. Properly speaking, the *hypostases* are not individually conscious, and therefore, according to Rahner's definition, they are not individually "persons." There is no intra-Trinitarian personal recipient for the Father's free self-communication. This critical oversight is compounded

---

insofar as he is unoriginate, we have already said that the Father himself has a manner of being given and of existing which distinguishes him from Son and Spirit, but which yet does not properly precede his relation to either of them" (ibid., 74).

25. Ibid., 85.

by the freedom that sustains this self-communication. For if the communication is free in the sense of mutual, willing, personal subjects accepting or rejecting each communication, then it seems to follow either (1) that God could possibly exist as something other than Trinity or (2) that there is a distinction between the immanent and the economic Trinity.[26] For Rahner to remain faithful to his theological methodology and Trinitarian axiom, something must give. Rahner says that in any self-communication, the addressee cannot be excluded.[27] But if the communication itself provides the distinction and diversity within the Trinity, there can be no intra-Trinitarian addressee. There is no intra-Trinitarian personal "other" when there is no personal distinction. The recipient of this self-communication, and therefore the impetus for intra-Trinitarian distinction, *must* be external.

This should cause us to consider more closely the nature of self-communication, which Rahner does by asking, "What do we mean by God's self-communication more precisely?"[28] His answer is telling: "To explain this we must look once again to the essence of man which becomes present basically and originally in transcendental experience."[29] In other words, divine

26. Ibid., 86.
27. Ibid., 88.
28. Rahner, *Foundations of Christian Faith*, 119.
29. Ibid. Rahner continues to insist that the immanent Trinity may be understood only by beginning with the economic Trinity: "We said that the doctrine of the Church speaks of *three* 'hypostases,' or 'subsistences.' It makes no attempt to explain independently from this context what a 'hypostasis' or 'subsistence' is. Hence to understand this concept theologically in this context we are referred to the concrete three, with whom we are concerned in our experience of salvation and also to our understanding of the one identical godhead (divine 'essence') which we attribute to the three. If we draw our inspiration from this starting point, hence also from the basic axiom of our theology of the Trinity, and if we are not simply content to use the two above words without further inquiry, then one way of expressing what we mean might be to say that these statements regarding the one same God, speak first ('economically') of three concrete ways of being given, of givenness, and then

self-communication cannot be understood strictly within God's *a se* existence. Man must be brought into consideration for divine self-communication to be comprehensible. And since the Son and Spirit are fundamentally self-communications of the Father, their existence is in some measure dependent upon humanity, the free personal recipients of the Father's essential self-communication. Because of the identification of the Father with the divine essence and the subjection of the Son's and the Spirit's personality to the Father-essence, Rahner resorts to a form of Sabellianism (patrimonism or modalistic monarchianism). Although he rejects such formulations, he fails to distinguish the consequences of his own view from them.

A Proposal: Perichoretic Personality

Relating persons within the Godhead is a complicated affair with a storied history. As the ecumenical creedal tradition developed, the language used to describe the Trinity evolved through the years. Rahner was right to recognize the various ways in which "person" has been used with reference to the Trinity. One's definition of personhood will either influence or be influenced significantly by one's Trinitarian theology. If we take the creedal formulations of Nicaea and Constantinople seriously, we must find a theological means for maintaining equal ultimacy among the *hypostases*. Father, Son, and Spirit are equally God, subsisting exhaustively in the divine essence such that there is no aspect of the divine essence that is impersonal or private to

---

('immanently') of three relative concrete ways of existing of the one and same God. The second expression can be understood only be referring it to the first, for it adds explicitly to the former that the 'immanent' actual possibility of this threefold way of being given is, despite God's free gratuitous trinitarian self-communication, forever given in God, belonging therefore necessarily and 'essentially' to him" (Rahner, *The Trinity*, 73–74).

any of the *hypostases*. God is not an impersonal essence that happens to have three persons attached to it. Neither is God three distinct and separate persons who happen to come together in an essence. God is triune. He is one and three, three in one.

To explain these matters, we turn to twentieth-century Reformed theologian Cornelius Van Til. Beginning with the triune God who has revealed himself, Van Til looks to Scripture and tradition in order to formulate an uncompromisingly Trinitarian theology. Like Rahner, Van Til believes that the formulations of the past were subject to misunderstanding.[30] But unlike Rahner, Van Til seeks to develop a Trinitarian theology that accounts for an independent, self-contained Trinity that may nevertheless relate to human beings personally. For Van Til, the absolute, self-contained Trinity is the foundation of all creation, and Van Til seeks to develop a Trinitarian theology that can account for the equal ultimacy of unity and diversity in the world, as well as meaningful interpersonal relationships. In this regard, Van Til sympathizes with the concerns of twentieth-century British and German absolute idealists, who insist that the world is an integrated system of subjects and objects. Knowledge of any single part presupposes knowledge of the whole.[31] To this, Van Til adds the work of the Boston personalists, who posit that such a "system" must be absolutely personal.[32] They maintain that for the world to be intelligible and personally dynamic, it must be bound together by absolute personality. For Van Til, the triune God, being a self-conscious personal being who is neither dependent upon nor derived from any other person or

30. Cornelius Van Til, *Introduction to Systematic Theology: Prolegomena and the Doctrines of Revelation, Scripture, and God*, 2nd ed. (Phillipsburg, NJ: P&R Publishing, 2007), 356–59, 363.

31. Van Til interacted primarily with the works of Bernard Bosanquet and F. H. Bradley on this point, but he also was wary of G. W. F. Hegel's influence.

32. A. C. Knudsen and Borden Parker Bowne were the most significant personalist thinkers for Van Til.

thing, acts as this absolute personal foundation. God is the perfect embodiment of personality, since his self-consciousness and essence are coterminous.[33]

For Van Til, nothing less than absolute personality is a sufficient metaphysical precondition for maintaining unity among diversity. Only God's absolute personality provides the necessary "personal atmosphere" required for human knowledge and, by extension, interpersonal relationships. Since man is finite, he is unable to grasp the entire system of knowledge. Neither can he serve as the universal ground of interpersonal relationships with his own personality. For Van Til, the only satisfactory personal and epistemological reference point is the self-contained, absolute, triune God revealed in Scripture:

> The problem of the one and the many, of the universal and the particular, of being and becoming, of analytical and synthetic reasoning, of the a priori and the a posteriori must be solved by an exclusive reference to the Trinity. The only alternative to this is to assume responsibility for trying to explain the whole of reality in temporal terms, and therefore with man as the ultimate point of reference.[34]

Van Til must find a way to hold the three persons of the Godhead together in one unified, yet exhaustively personal,

---

33. "If, in God, being and essence are really coterminous, we have before us an absolute personality. There is then no distinction between absoluteness and personality. God does not merely have a personality, but is absolute personality. This implies that he is the absolute originator of any being that may exist beside himself. And this in turn implies that the mind of man must, in its interpretive activity, think God's thoughts after him" (Van Til, *Introduction to Systematic Theology*, 346). Van Til maintains that "if God is left out of the picture it is up to the human mind to furnish the unity that must bind together the diversity of factual existence" (Cornelius Van Til, *A Survey of Christian Epistemology*, 2nd ed. [Phillipsburg, NJ: Presbyterian and Reformed, 1980], 216).

34. Van Til, *A Survey of Christian Epistemology*, 96–97.

entity. Like Rahner, Van Til is aware of the danger of positing an abstract personal essence.[35] Van Til avoids this problem with his doctrine of *perichoresis*. Because man is finite, and because unity and diversity are equally ultimate within the Godhead, whenever we think of the one, we are inevitably drawn to the three. And whenever we think of the three, we are inevitably drawn to the one. This "Nazianzen Circle" reminds us of God's incomprehensibility. As we indicated earlier, several interpreters have interacted with Gregory's statement, but not all have done so through the lens of *perichoresis*. This doctrine addresses the shortcomings of Rahner's approach.

Although contemporary formulations differ, most formulations of *perichoresis* understand it as the mutual indwelling or cohering of each *hypostasis* with the other *hypostases* and the divine essence. But since theologians differ on the definition of "person," this lowest common denominator definition of *perichoresis* leaves much to be desired. As detailed earlier in our study, Rahner acknowledges traditional distinctions among the *hypostases* in accordance with their respective personal properties. For the Western tradition, the Father is unbegotten, the Son is begotten, and the Spirit proceeds from both the Father and the Son. Rahner, on the other hand, understands the Father as unoriginate, and the Spirit and Son as twin aspects of the

---

35. "We do assert that God, that is, the whole Godhead, is one person. We have noted how each attribute is coextensive with the being of God. We are compelled to maintain this in order to avoid the notion of an uninterpreted being of some sort" (Van Til, *Introduction to Systematic Theology*, 363; see also p. 363n45). When Van Til refers to the "whole Godhead" as "one person," he is speaking in a different sense than that of the ecumenical creeds. God is not three hypostases as well as one hypostasis, thereby making four hypostases. Rather, the Father, Son, and Holy Spirit indwell one another exhaustively, such that we may address the "whole Godhead" personally. We may pray to God, that is the Trinity, and refer to "him" rather than "it," because "he" is exhaustively personal. As triune, he knows and loves. Van Til might have avoided much of the criticism he has received simply by speaking of God as triunely personal, rather than as "one person and three persons."

Father's eternal self-communication. The distinction between them pertains to how they subsist in the divine essence, that is, how they are self-communicated. The distinction does not involve personality through self-consciousness, self-awareness, or agency. For both the Western tradition and Rahner, relating divine personality to all *hypostases* is a challenge. However, the solution to these "personal" problems is not, as some might suggest, to seal hermetically the definition of "person" from either the unity or the diversity in the Godhead. It will not suffice to say that we may speak of personality only with specific reference to a *hypostasis*, because those very *hypostases* subsist exhaustively in the divine essence. Van Til's use of *perichoresis* provides an avenue for approaching these difficult questions, for it affords God the means to be personal, both in his unity and his diversity.[36] This is the genius of his approach. Van Til consciously builds upon the Trinitarian theology of Charles Hodge as a theological means of protecting against an abstract *ousia*. Hodge, for example, understands that Christians pray to and otherwise speak of God in personal categories. God thinks, wills, loves, and acts. At the same time, Christians also rightly pray with reference to the Father, Son, and Spirit as distinct persons. They recognize that each member of the Trinity also exhibits the same personal traits that the entire Godhead exhibits as a unity. For Hodge, "The three persons are one God; one not only in substance, but in knowledge, will, and power."[37] Tipton notes that Hodge's language regarding the unity of God moves beyond substance terminology.[38] Many theologians have no theological means

36. For a thorough explication and defense of Van Til's theology of Trinitarian personality in light of *perichoresis*, see Lane G. Tipton, "The Triune Personal God: Trinitarian Theology in the Thought of Cornelius Van Til," PhD diss., Westminster Theological Seminary, 2004.

37. Charles Hodge, *Systematic Theology* (Peabody, MA: Hendrickson, 1999), 1:462. See also, Tipton, "The Triune Personal God," 52.

38. Tipton, "The Triune Personal God," 45.

for negotiating this issue, and so they stop short of full equal ultimacy. They recognize the individual *hypostases* as persons, but speak of the unity of the Godhead only with respect to the divine essence. That is, they do not unite the persons or personality directly. Hodge, however, relates these three persons exhaustively through *perichoresis*. While Hodge is quite helpful, he still recognized unity only with regard to knowledge, will, and power.[39]

Van Til pushes Hodge's doctrine of *perichoresis* toward even greater consistency. For if the *hypostases* share equally and exhaustively in the knowledge, will, and power of the divine essence, while also remaining distinct, there must somehow also be three instances of knowledge, will, and power. God is uni-conscious, but if there is absolute cotermineity of the divine attributes in addition to meaningful distinctions among the *hypostases*, he must in some way also be tri-conscious.[40] At this point, Rahner immediately raises the charge of tritheism. For Rahner, to claim three centers of self-consciousness is to claim three gods. But one must appreciate the implications of *perichoresis* and what it means for the *hypostases* to subsist in the divine essence exhaustively. The affirmation of three perichoretically related self-consciousnesses should not be understood as the affirmation of three *independent* centers of self-consciousness. Father, Son, and Spirit each exhibit personality, and all three are conscious of their personal distinctions, but they do so as *hypostases* who exhaustively indwell one another.[41] To avoid

---

39. "As the essence of the Godhead is common to the several persons, they have a common intelligence, will, and power. There are not in God three intelligences, three wills, three efficiencies. The Three are one God, and therefore have one mind and will. This intimate union was expressed in the Greek Church by the word περιχώρησις, (*perichōrēsis*), which the Latin words *inexistentia*, *inhabitatio*, and *intercommunio*, were used to explain" (Hodge, *Systematic Theology*, 1:461).

40. Van Til, *Introduction to Systematic Theology*, 346–48.

41. Tipton distills the personal aspects of unity and diversity in this formulation

confusion—or worse, heterodoxy—it would be better to speak of God as *triunely* conscious than as tri-conscious or even as singularly conscious *simpliciter*. He is always and everywhere three in one, triune.

Through *perichoresis*, unity and diversity remain equally ultimate. The *hypostases* indwell one another exhaustively, while at the same time remaining distinct. Through *perichoresis*, the *hypostases* have inexhaustibly meaningful relationships with each other. Each *hypostasis* is an intra-Trinitarian, personal, *and absolute* "other." Maintaining three persons in this manner does not result in tritheism, because the persons mutually and exhaustively indwell one another *without remainder*. There is no private aspect of the essence relative to the *hypostases* nor of the *hypostases* relative to each other. Hence, there are not three independent centers of conscious activity. While each *hypostasis* is self-conscious, together they inhabit the same center of consciousness in the divine essence through *perichoresis*.

Van Til sees his formulation of *perichoresis* as an expository advancement of creedal Trinitarianism.[42] He affirms both the creedal formulae and their organic advancement in Reformed Trinitarianism. For Van Til, *perichoresis* relates unity and diversity absolutely without resorting to tritheism or Sabellianism. The *hypostases* indwell one another in such a way that the divine essence is itself one self-conscious, willing agent. However, genuine distinctions remain according to the personal properties or modes of subsistence of each *hypostasis*. The Father is eternally unbegotten and distinct from the Son, who is eternally begotten

---

of *perichoresis*: "For Van Til, then, the persons of the Godhead are not artificially attached to an impersonal essence, since that would involve three distinct and *independent* centers of consciousness within the Trinity. Instead, we ought to say that God is an "absolute personality" in such a way that the genuine distinctions among the persons are not obliterated or compromised" ("The Triune Personal God," 49).

42. Van Til, *Introduction to Systematic Theology*, 19–20.

from the Father, and the Spirit is distinct from both the Father and the Son in that he eternally proceeds from both the Father and the Son (John 15:26; 20:22; 1 Cor. 2:10–13). Each *hypostasis* is a self-conscious, willing agent. This is no insignificant mystery, and at this point Van Til appeals to divine incomprehensibility.[43] The principles of equal ultimacy, absolute personality, and *perichoresis* form the foundation of this Trinitarian theology. Each principle is fundamental. Should any principle be compromised, the unity or the diversity will be absolutized, and then the intelligibility and the personal atmosphere of the world will be sacrificed.

Conclusion

Rahner's notion of *perichoresis* begins with an unsatisfactory understanding of the *hypostases*, because it stresses the unity of the Godhead above the diversity. His formulation of *perichoresis* stops short of exhaustive hypostatic penetration within the divine essence. Without understanding the eternal ontic status of Father, Son, and Spirit, Rahner cannot rightly formulate a doctrine of coinherence. He must choose between personal unity and personal diversity; he cannot have both. As a consequence, he must resort to panentheism, forms of Monarchianism, or Nestorianism. The formulation of *perichoresis* advanced by Cornelius Van Til is one solution, but Rahner's Eastern doctrine of the Trinity and Trinitarian personality precludes it. He cannot admit equal ultimacy in the Godhead without compromising his theology of personal self-communication.

Having traced the thread of Trinitarian personality throughout Rahner's theology and now having demonstrated its

---

43. See also Lane G. Tipton, "The Function of Perichoresis and the Divine Incomprehensibility," *Westminster Theological Journal* 64 (2002): 289–306.

significant flaws, we may next evaluate Rahner's understanding of the Trinitarian aspects of grace. The triune God desires to give the gift of himself, but Rahner, on his own terms, is unable to account for a fully Trinitarian gift.

7

A PROPOSAL FOR COVENANTAL IMAGE CONFORMITY

Having detailed several problematic features of Rahner's theological methodology and his theology of Trinitarian personality, we may now explore their effects upon his understanding of ontological self-communication. The two are intimately related. If God gives the gift of himself through an interpersonal exchange with humanity, the nature of the giver has everything to do with the nature of the gift. This aspect of the present study stands to offer the most to contemporary Reformed theology. Whereas Cornelius Van Til developed a helpful theology that addresses the challenges inherent in Rahner's proposal, we must do more originally constructive work before we can offer meaningful criticisms of Rahner's doctrine of divine self-communication. The landscape is unsettled at the moment. Debates rage regarding the nature of Trinitarian theology, but at least the issues are well defined. However, in terms of confessionally Reformed

scholarship on divinization, deification, participation, glorification, and related subjects, scholars are still identifying the issues,
not solidifying a response to them. So before explicating the
implications of Rahner's theology of divine self-communication,
we will offer guidelines for developing a theology of glorification that accounts for the type of perichoretic personality we
proposed in the previous chapter. This chapter is offered as a
Reformed alternative to Rahner's proposal. It is not a full-fledged
defense of a Reformed critique of the Roman Catholic theological
tradition. For that, we would have to undertake an extensive
treatment of the medieval tradition to demonstrate how the
Reformed tradition differs from the Scotist trajectory that
Rahner follows. Such a project would far exceed the limits of this
present work. Nonetheless, we hope this study will lay a modest
foundation for such a work and for meaningful dialogue between
Reformed and Catholic theologians on these issues.

In light of recent Reformed scholarship, the salvific benefits
most closely connected to Rahner's understanding of ontological self-communication are union with Christ and glorification.
Justification and sanctification receive much attention in
Reformed discussions of the *ordo salutis*, and union with Christ
has become a fixture in the contemporary literature, but glorification remains a rather vague concept in the minds of many.
Thorough biblical-theological definitions are noticeably lacking
in the literature on soteriology, and developed understandings
of precisely what is communicated in glorification are rarer still.
Many times, glorification is simply identified with future bodily
resurrection, but, as we will see, Scripture speaks of the bestowal
of glory in a fuller and more diverse sense.[1] The threads of a

---

1. Basic treatments of glorification include Michael Horton, *The Christian Faith:
A Systematic Theology for Pilgrims on the Way* (Grand Rapids: Zondervan, 2011),
688–89; Wayne Grudem, *Systematic Theology: An Introduction to Biblical Doctrine*
(Leicester: Inter-Varsity Press; Grand Rapids: Zondervan, 2000), 828–39, 1242–43;

robust response to Rahner are present within Reformed teaching, but they have not yet been woven together into a tightly knit fabric. Before turning our attention to Rahner's view, we will seek to advance a doctrine of glorification that draws particularly upon the theological contributions of Geerhardus Vos, Herman Ridderbos, Meredith Kline, and Richard B. Gaffin Jr.[2] Following a positive construction of the doctrine, we will seek to put it to use polemically against the theology of Karl Rahner. Although this study will necessarily be brief, we are optimistic that it will suggest areas for future critical dialogue with Eastern Orthodoxy and the growing number of emerging deification and divinization theologies.

J. van Genderen and W. H. Velema, *Concise Reformed Dogmatics* (Phillipsburg, NJ: P&R Publishing, 2008), 495, 858, 868; Robert L. Reymond, *A New Systematic Theology of the Christian Faith* (Nashville: T. Nelson, 1998), 795–801. Bavinck recognizes a broader concept behind Paul's use of the word ἐδόξασεν (*edoxasen*) in Rom. 8:30, but still speaks of glorification properly as the resurrection of the body on the last day. See Herman Bavinck, *Reformed Dogmatics*, vol. 3, *Sin and Salvation in Christ*, ed. John Bolt, trans. John Vriend (Grand Rapids: Baker Academic, 2006), 594–95. Frame recognizes an eschatological dimension to glorification, exhibited in present and future aspects. See John M. Frame, *Systematic Theology: An Introduction to Christian Belief* (Phillipsburg, NJ: P&R Publishing, 2013), 1009–13. God's glory is revealed in the things that have been made and climactically through his Son, Jesus Christ. He bestows his glory and honor upon his people in creation and then in redemption and consummation. The concept of glorification—or, more generally, the bestowal of God's glory—includes bodily resurrection, but is also much more. For example, see Ex. 28:2, 40; 40:34; Pss. 3:3; 8:5; 21:5; 84:11; Prov. 3:35; 8:18; 15:33; 29:23; Isa. 6:3; 43:7; 60:1; Ezek. 39:21; Hab. 2:14; Hag. 2:7, 9; Zech. 2:5; Matt. 17:2; John 1:14; 2:11; 5:44; 7:18; 8:54; 13:31, 32; 15:8; 17:1, 4, 5, 10, 24; Rom. 2:7, 10; 5:2; 8:17–19, 21, 30; 9:4, 23; 1 Cor. 6:20; 15:43; 2 Cor. 3:7–11, 18; 4:6; Phil. 3:21; Heb. 2:10; 1 Peter 4:13–14; 5:4; 2 Peter 1:3.

2. The following works are particularly helpful for constructing a Reformed theology of glorification: Geerhardus Vos, *Biblical Theology: Old and New Testaments* (Edinburgh/Carlisle, PA: Banner of Truth, 1975); Geerhardus Vos, *The Pauline Eschatology* (Phillipsburg, NJ: P&R Publishing, 1994); Herman N. Ridderbos, *Paul: An Outline of His Theology* (Grand Rapids: Eerdmans, 1977); Meredith G. Kline, *Images of the Spirit* (Eugene, OR: Wipf and Stock, 1999); Richard B. Gaffin Jr., *Resurrection and Redemption: A Study in Paul's Soteriology*, 2nd ed. (Phillipsburg, NJ: Presbyterian and Reformed, 1987).

The vocabularies used by traditional Reformed dogmaticians and twentieth-century Catholic theologians are quite different, even though all the traditional Reformed *loci* are addressed, without conspicuous exception, in Rahner's theological corpus. Whereas Reformed, and to some extent evangelical, theologians speak of glorification in the context of a detailed *ordo salutis*, Catholic theologians, such as Rahner, speak generally of receiving God's grace in the beatific vision.[3] The latter tend to emphasize the unity of God's program of consummation rather than its constituent parts. Justification is a transformative benefit, according to official Catholic teaching, and strictly forensic notions of pardon from sin are alien to Catholic dogmatics. Instead of sharply distinguishing between forensic and renovative categories, as the Reformed have, Catholic dogmaticians such as Rahner prefer to treat all of salvation from the perspective of the whole—in one graced sum that comes to consummation when Christ returns and believers are raised imperishable. Even though these approaches seem widely divergent and have underscored the division between Catholics and Protestants since the sixteenth century, official Catholic teaching in general, and Karl Rahner's writings in particular, provide ample opportunity for dialogue with Reformed thought. The renewed interest in union with Christ and theologies of deification and divinization have only served to bring these two traditions into closer orbit. Yet while the vocabulary and theological issues with which these theologians deal are

3. A sequential approach to the *ordo salutis* began with Theodore Beza's "table" and was further solidified in William Perkins's "golden chain." See William Perkins, *A Golden Chain: or, The Description of Theology Containing the Order of the Causes of Salvation and Damnation, according to God's Word*, Puritan Reprints (Port St. Lucie, FL: Solid Ground Christian Books, 2010). This theological tradition is echoed in contemporary theologies (such as the basic views referenced above) that treat glorification at the end of this sequence of salvific events. Rahner's view is helpfully summarized in Karl Rahner, "Beatific Vision," in *Encyclopedia of Theology: The Concise Sacramentum Mundi*, ed. Karl Rahner (New York: Seabury, 1975), 78–80.

converging, the underlying biblical, systematic, and philosophical assumptions remain worlds apart. With these opportunities and provisos in mind, we will begin to construct a Reformed theology of glorification.

Glorification Themes in Scripture

Glorification is the bestowal of divine glory upon God's people. In short, God's glory is his essence, the sum of his eternal attributes. But for a more thorough understanding, we ought to look first to Paul's words in Romans 1:20:

> For his invisible attributes, namely, his eternal power and divine nature, have been clearly perceived, ever since the creation of the world, in the things that have been made.

> τὰ γὰρ ἀόρατα αὐτοῦ ἀπὸ κτίσεως κόσμου τοῖς ποιήμασιν νοούμενα καθορᾶται, ἥ τε ἀΐδιος αὐτοῦ δύναμις καὶ θειότης.

> *ta gar aorata autou apo ktiseōs kosmou tois poiēmasin nooumena kathoratai, hē te aidios autou dynamis kai theiotēs.*

God's glory is evident in the things that have been made, because they reveal and manifest his being. Created things disclose his eternal attributes, not as original sources of divine being, but as derivative demonstrators of God's being in accommodated form. This is true especially of man's constitutive being. Basic to the notion of Christian anthropology is the teaching that Adam was created in the image of God. Image is bound up with the notion of God's glory, because man manifests God's glory precisely *as* image. Much has been written regarding man being created in the image of God, but little has connected that image to an eschatological conception of bestowing glory.

Meredith Kline is a welcome exception. Although he relates image and glory, Kline distinguishes slightly between the two as "twin models in the Bible for expressing man's likeness to the divine Original. If they are to be distinguished, the distinction might be that image-likeness is reproduction of the original and glory-likeness is reflection of the original."[4] Both conceptions have an eschatological dimension. Original, archetypal glory is comprehensive, and when man is made to be like the glorious God and reflect the divine glory as created copies (ectypally), we should anticipate this glory encompassing all aspects of human existence. This is precisely what Kline develops:

> Under the concept of man as the glory-image of God the Bible includes functional (or official), formal (or physical), and ethical components, corresponding to the composition of the archetypal Glory. Functional glory-likeness is man's likeness to God in the possession of official authority and in the exercise of dominion. Ethical glory is reflection of the holiness, righteousness, and truth of the divine Judge (not just the presence of a moral faculty of any religious orientation whatsoever). And formal-physical glory-likeness is man's bodily reflection of the theophanic and incarnate Glory.[5]

This "glory-image" is thoroughly eschatological. It was given as good, but not as perfect (in the sense of being complete). This dynamic is formally similar to Rahner's notion of elevating grace. God blessed man with his glory as created, but he had an eschatological goal intended for this image—one that would be realized in consummated union and communion with the triune God. Nonetheless, the glory with which the protological son was

4. Kline, *Images of the Spirit*, 30.
5. Ibid., 31.

invested did not remain in its pristine form.[6] Adam fell from glory when he sinned by eating of the tree of the knowledge of good and evil. As a result, he no longer imaged properly. The image was not lost entirely, but it was damaged in all of its aspects. Adam lost dominion when he failed to keep the garden pure, by succumbing to the serpent (Genesis 3). He was darkened in his understanding through the knowledge of sin (Rom. 1:21; Eph. 4:18). And finally, his flesh was subjected to corruption and death (Rom. 5:12; 6:23). Although the glory-image in man in some sense remains (see Gen. 9:6), it has been altered significantly.

This basic pattern of bearing God's glory-image was recapitulated at a typological level for the nation of Israel. Like the protological son before them, the nation of Israel bore God's glory as typological son (Exod. 4:22; 28:2, 40; 40:34; Ps. 3:3; Zech. 2:5). As a type, the nation exhibited a form of the glory that anticipated the eschatological glory yet to be recovered and consummated. The glory of the nation was most closely identified first with the tabernacle and the premier prophet, Moses, and later with the temple. Second Corinthians 3–4 explains this glory within the typological period of redemptive history. Here Paul focuses on the glory of God shining in Moses's face. This was a manifestation of God's own glory. It was so significant that Moses had to place a veil over his face so the Israelites would not look upon the glory directly and perish. But as great as this glory was, it was only provisional and faded. It was not original to Moses and depended upon him going before the Lord in the tent of meeting (Exod. 34:29–35; 2 Cor. 3:7–18). Typological glory was provisional by nature, but even it was forfeited. Just as Adam

---

6. The word *protological* refers to the covenant-historical age from creation to man's fall into sin. Adam is the premier "son" of this age. Typology characterizes the time after the fall leading up to the life, death, and resurrection of Christ. The nation of Israel represents God's son in this covenant-historical era. Eschatology refers to the end and consummation of all things. Jesus Christ is the eschatological Son of God.

lost the protological glory when he fell in the garden, so also this typological glory did not remain. The nation of Israel, after repeatedly breaking covenant, "fell" from glory and was exiled into Babylon. In climactic conclusion to God's typological presence with the national image bearer, the glory of the Lord left the temple (Ezek. 10:18; cf. 1 Sam. 4:21).

Even after two forfeitures—protological and typological—God's original plan of glory bestowal and of consummated union and communion was still possible. In God's plan of redemption, the eschatological son would come to redeem his people (Gen. 3:15; cf. Rom. 5:12–15; 1 Cor. 15:20ff.). But this image bearer differs markedly from the previous two. His experience of glory and his mode of displaying it are categorically different from those of Adam, Israel, and the rest of humanity. Christ is not simply a reflection of the divine glory, but the origin and source of it, the perfect image of the invisible God (Col. 1:15; cf. John 14:4; 17:5; Heb. 1:3). Although being the eternal God and partaking in the fullness of triune glory, he took the form of a servant (Phil. 2:7). He had no form or majesty that we should look at him, or any beauty that we should desire him (Isa. 53:2). Rather, he humbled himself for a servant's life of suffering unto glory. The hypostatic union of divine and human natures in the person of Christ has great significance for the bestowal of glory to God's people. His glory is original to his person and divine nature, but changes in relation to his human nature. This understanding of glorification, refracted through hypostatic union, offers a paradigm for understanding how glory is bestowed upon God's people who come to be united to Christ. Christ's life between incarnation and resurrected glory was a redemptive-historical movement that elevated his human nature to a consummative glory in closer relationship to his eternal glory as eternal Son of God. This eschatological trajectory toward Christ's glorious climax was seen in stages throughout his earthly ministry. It was manifested when the angels confessed glory to God at Christ's birth (Luke 2:14), and it was demonstrated as Christ performed miracles. It broke through even more strikingly at his transfiguration (Matt. 17:1–9; Mark 9:2–8; Luke 9:28–36; cf. 2 Peter 1:16–18).

The glory demonstrated by Christ, the eschatological son, is not substantially different from the glory demonstrated by the protological or typological son. It is the same divine glory, but the mode and fullness of the manifestation differs. This can be understood better by comparing Moses's glorious transfiguration to Christ's. Paul connects Moses's transfiguration to Christ's original glory. Believers are made to behold and see (κατοπτρίζω, *katoptrizō*) this glory through the Spirit in union with Christ (2 Cor. 3:18). In the transfiguration, the eternal glory of the Son breaks through in redemptive history with a foretaste of the eschatological glory that will adorn him in the fullness of his kingdom for all eternity (Pss. 68:18; 110; Heb. 10:13). This is Trinitarian glory. The Son possessed it with the Father from all eternity, but he is also functionally identified with the Spirit when his glory is manifested through his resurrection (1 Cor. 15:45; 2 Cor. 3:17). If Christ came to restore the originally promised Trinitarian glory to his people by accomplishing redemption and offering a redemptive-historical paradigm to them, it behooves us to consider how the transfiguration might be proleptic of the believer's experience.[7] It is also necessary to understand the significant difference between Christ's original glory as the eternal Son of God and believers' manifestation of derivative glory, which they receive as part of the body of Christ.

---

7. The operative word μεταμορφόω (*metamorphoō*) appears in Matt. 17:2; Mark 9:2; Rom. 12:2; 2 Cor. 3:18. In particular, 2 Cor. 3:18 connects Christ's glory with believers' glory. The transfiguration is an important redemptive-historical event that sheds light on the beatific vision, though there will necessarily be differences between Christ's and the believer's experience, since Jesus is the eternal Son of God. His glory is original. The glory of his people is and will be derivative.

For this, we should consider the relationship between glory and transformation within the context of union with Christ.

Christ bestows his glory through a mystical and *covenantal* bond. By contrast, Rahner identifies the hypostatic union as the conduit of *ontological* self-communication in the beatific vision. The nature of a mystical, glorious bond between Christ and his people is described in 1 Corinthians 15:20, 23. Paul invokes the agricultural term ἀπαρχή (firstfruits, *aparchē*) to characterize this relationship of glory, which culminates in resurrection. Resurrection is the eschatological manifestation of glory, and Christ's resurrection is organically connected to the resurrection of those who follow in the harvest. According to this conception, the resurrection of Christ and the resurrection of his people are not separate events. There is a single harvest, which is reaped in two stages.[8] This has tremendous implications for the doctrine of union with Christ.[9] For if Christ is organically connected with his people in his resurrection, and if Christ's resurrection brought him glory, then union between Christ and his people must play an important role in their glorification.[10] The means of glorification must be circumscribed by several programmatic biblical texts. One is Romans 8:29, which identifies the purpose of predestination as bringing the elect into conformity to Christ's

---

8. Gaffin, *Resurrection and Redemption*, 35–36.

9. The scope of this study will not permit us to ask what kind of metaphysical significance we can ascribe to the apostle's use of ἀπαρχή (*aparchē*). In short, we must maintain that it is a spiritual union, that is, the work of the Holy Spirit. The bond with Adam is natural, but the bond with Christ is spiritual. For further study, see John Murray, *The Imputation of Adam's Sin* (Grand Rapids: Eerdmans, 1959), 22ff. In both cases, the bond is covenantal. The means of our incorporation into Adam is natural birth, but the ultimate reason that his sin is imputed to all who descend from him by ordinary generation is the covenant that God established with Adam in the garden. Humanity's foundational problem is ethical-covenantal, not biological.

10. Ralph Martin points out that μεταμορφούμεθα (*metamorphoumetha*) in 2 Cor. 3:18 "strongly suggests a link with Christ as God's 'image' who is the prototype" (*2 Corinthians*, Word Biblical Commentary 40 [Waco, TX: Word Books, 1986], 71).

image, so that he could become the firstborn of many brothers. In other words, the resurrected Christ becomes the prototype for a glorified family resemblance.[11] As significant as this text is for an overall program of covenantal image conformity, perhaps the key passage as it pertains to Rahner's particular concerns is 2 Peter 1:4. We will now turn to a more detailed treatment of this passage with a view to providing an overall framework for understanding God's gift of himself in glory.

An Aeonic Interpretation of 2 Peter 1:4

Theologians interested in various forms of divinization and deification often appeal to 2 Peter 1:4 in support of their views. In this passage, Peter speaks of partaking of the divine nature. Rahner references it with regard to the metaphysical attributes of God.[12] The language of 2 Peter 1:4 is unique in Scripture, and its similarity to philosophical terminology has given theologians the opportunity to interpret the text according to metaphysical rather than ethical considerations.[13] For instance, one interpretation views Peter as teaching that believers participate in the "energies" of God.

11. According to 2 Cor. 3:18, Christ's people are being transformed from one degree of glory to another. The transformation does not occur in an instant. Rather, it is progressive (ἀπὸ δόξης εἰς δόξαν, *apo doxēs eis doxan*). This differentiates the transformation of 2 Cor. 3:18 from the transformation spoken of in 1 Cor. 15:52, which occurs "in a moment, in the twinkling of an eye" (ἐν ἀτόμῳ, ἐν ῥιπῇ ὀφθαλμοῦ, *en atomō, en rhipē ophthalmou*). We should note that while these are two aspects of giving life, the life that is given is the same. It is life in Christ via personal, spiritual, and eschatological union (Eph. 1:3).

12. Karl Rahner, "Theos in the New Testament," in *Theological Investigations*, vol. 1, trans. Cornelius Ernst (Baltimore: Helicon, 1961), 112.

13. For a sampling of views, see Michael J. Christensen and Jeffery A. Wittung, *Partakers of the Divine Nature: The History and Development of Deification in the Christian Traditions* (Grand Rapids: Baker Academic, 2008). Ben C. Blackwell describes Cyril of Alexandria's use of 2 Peter 1:4 to advance a theology of deification in *Christosis: Pauline Soteriology in Light of Deification in Irenaeus and Cyril of Alexandria*, Wissenschaftliche Untersuchungen zum Neuen Testament 2/314 (Tübingen: Mohr

Another views Peter as teaching that believers will indeed become gods.[14] Defenders of such interpretations appeal to Psalm 90:2; Hosea 11:9; John 10:34; Galatians 4:8; and for textual warrant. In some measure, this may be what Rahner presents with his notion of divine ontological self-communication. The task for Reformed theologians is to develop a robust theology of glorification without compromising the Creator-creature distinction or resorting to metaphysical speculation. These concerns should be kept in the background when considering Peter's words in 2 Peter 1:4:

> by which he has granted to us his precious and very great promises, so that through them you may become partakers of the divine nature, having escaped from the corruption that is in the world because of sinful desire.

> δι᾽ ὧν τὰ τίμια καὶ μέγιστα ἡμῖν ἐπαγγέλματα δεδώρηται, ἵνα διὰ τούτων γένησθε θείας κοινωνοὶ φύσεως, ἀποφυγόντες τῆς ἐν τῷ κόσμῳ ἐν ἐπιθυμίᾳ φθορᾶς.[15]

Siebeck, 2011), 86–88. Reformed theologians have devoted little effort to developing a metaphysics of glorification. Whether or not such a development would be a positive metaphysical definition or simply a biblical-theological set of guidelines and boundaries for metaphysical speculation, the theological product is absent.

14. Eastern Orthodoxy distinguishes between God's essence and his energies. According to the Fifth Council of Constantinople (1351), the distinction is not intended to compromise divine simplicity. Yet the distinction is generally regarded as real. Moreover, the energies of God are uncreated, and the term "deity" may properly be ascribed to them. Mormonism teaches a form of polytheism. While quite distinct from one another, both Eastern Orthodoxy and Mormonism teach a metaphysical view of transformation. Current scholarship has demonstrated that metaphysical views of transformation are also finding a foothold in the Reformed orbit of thought, particularly in Calvin studies such as Carl Mosser, "The Greatest Possible Blessing: Calvin and Deification," *Scottish Journal of Theology* 55, no. 1 (February 1, 2002): 36–57. Mosser is certainly not advancing a view such as Eastern Orthodox *theosis*, but he is advancing a view of deification that many confessional Reformed thinkers would find uncomfortably close to blurring the Creator-creature distinction.

15. This and all other references to the Greek New Testament refer to Nestle-Aland, *Novum Testamentum Graece*, 28th ed.

*di' hōn ta timia kai megista hēmin epangelmata dedōrētai, hina
dia toutōn genēsthe theias koinōnoi physeōs, apophygontes tēs en tō
kosmō en epithymia phthoras.*

Interpreting "Nature"

Peter's use of φύσις (*physis*) is of greatest importance, since
one's understanding of the use of this word will govern the interpretation of this text. It is common to find φύσις in ancient Greek,
even in Greek philosophy. For instance, it demonstrates a broad
semantic range in such works as Plato's *Phaedo* and *Cratylus*.[16]
One way to consider φύσις is in terms of essentialism or a substance metaphysic. In this sense, believers come to participate in
the divine life by sharing in the divine essence. In another sense,
φύσις may be understood as referring to divine qualities that God
"takes to himself" by condescending to relate to his creation.[17]
In such a view, believers could assume properties that God has
assumed in condescension. Sound exegesis should direct us
toward one of these options, a middle position, or perhaps an
entirely different type of understanding. For that, we must begin
with the use of this word in the Bible.

Although φύσις (*physis*) occurs four times in the Apocrypha
(4 Macc. 5:8–9; 13:27; Wisd. 19:20), Romans 2:27 is the
only other biblical instance of φύσις in the feminine singular
(φύσεως), *physeōs*). The word does appear, however, in other
forms throughout the New Testament. It demonstrates a broad
semantic domain, which ranges from the sense of "physical"
(Rom. 2:27) and ethnicity (Gal. 2:15) to "kind" or "type"

16. Thesaurus Linguae Graecae, "φύσις." University of California, accessed
December 1, 2011, http://stephanus.tlg.uci.edu/inst/textsearch.

17. For a treatment of this approach to God's relationship to creation, see K. Scott
Oliphint, *God with Us: Divine Condescension and the Attributes of God* (Wheaton, IL:
Crossway, 2011). In this particular work, man does not participate in God's nature.
Rather, God comes to participate in the same contingency that characterizes human
nature by assuming covenantal properties even prior to the incarnation.

(James 3:7). Furthermore, Romans 1:26 speaks about homosexuality as an act that is contrary to *nature*. Later, Paul uses φύσις in Romans 2:14 to speak of Gentiles who *by nature* do the works of the law. Then in Romans 11:21, 24, he speaks of ethnic Jews as *natural* branches, that is, those belonging to the people of God by virtue of their physical birth and Israel's national election. First Corinthians 11:14 even declares that *nature* teaches that long hair on a man is a disgrace. Each of these passages helps to inform the use of φύσις in 2 Peter 1:4, but Galatians 4:8 might be the closest Paul comes to a metaphysical sense. Paul refers there to those who "were enslaved to those that by nature are not gods."[18] Each of these uses is important to the respective context of Paul's arguments. Not one, however, is principally concerned with Paul's theology of eschatological transformation.

The Pauline use of φύσις (*physis*) is often aeonic, pertaining to the relationship of this age (aeon) to the age to come. This is evident in passages like Ephesians 2:3, which speaks of those fallen in Adam as "by nature children of wrath." In this type of use, φύσις refers to one's basic identity and the characteristics that are concomitant with that identity. This is likely the sense in which Peter uses the word. He invokes an aeonic consideration in chapter 3 of his second epistle, where he speaks about "the last days" (2 Peter 3:3) and of "the world that then existed" (2 Peter 3:6). He divides world history into three fundamental orders or ages. The flood destroyed the world that then existed (v. 6). The present world will be burned up in a purifying fire of judgment (vv. 10, 12) and will yield to "new heavens and a new earth in

---

18. Luke records Paul making a similar comment in Acts 14:15. The people of Lystra witnessed Barnabas and Paul performing miracles, and as a result they identified Barnabas as Zeus and Paul as Hermes. But Paul says, "Men, why are you doing these things? We also are men, of like nature with you, and we bring you good news, that you should turn from these vain things to a living God, who made the heaven and the earth and the sea and all that is in them" (Acts 14:15).

which righteousness dwells" (v. 13). This aeonic framework is being employed in 1:4, where he speaks of the corruption that is "in the world" (ἐν τῷ κόσμῳ, *en tō kosmō*) in a manner similar to Paul's aeonic language in Ephesians 1:10 and Colossians 1:16 (cf. Col. 3:2). In both places, Paul speaks of things in the heavens (ἐν/ἐπὶ τοῖς οὐρανοῖς, *en/epi tois ouranois*) and things on the earth (ἐπὶ τῆς γῆς, *epi tēs gēs*). Peter's ἐν τῷ κόσμῳ invokes a similar division of world orders. Furthermore, 1 Peter speaks of "the time of your exile" (1:17), "the revelation of Jesus Christ" (1 Peter 1:6–8), and the manifestation of Christ "in the last times" (1:20). In so doing, Peter clearly exhibits an aeonic mindset similar to Paul's. Therefore, it is natural to read Peter's second epistle with a two-age eschatology in mind. This paradigm should then condition what it means to participate in the divine nature. Hence, we should interpret partaking of the divine nature to mean sharing in some characteristic in accord with a heavenly mode of existence in the age to come. This aeonic sense is the sense in which Peter employs φύσις in 2 Peter 1:4 to advance his theology of eschatological transformation.

Incorruptibility

It is indeed surprising that this passage has been used as a foothold for all manner of philosophical speculation, particularly since Peter qualifies his intent in the very next phrase. There he writes that partaking of the divine nature results in "having escaped from the corruption that is in the world because of sinful desire" (ἀποφυγόντες τῆς ἐν τῷ κόσμῳ ἐν ἐπιθυμίᾳ φθορᾶς, *apophygontes tēs en tō kosmō en epithymia phthoras*). Partaking of the divine nature then involves a new mode of existence, namely, one characteristic of a new age. Thus, if partaking of the divine nature is a matter of escaping corruption, we must then ask when this happens. Surely believers remain subject to physical decay and eventual death in this life. Yet they also have already received new life in Christ and have been liberated from sin's corruption (Rom. 6:1–11), not simply its guilt. This evokes the tension characteristic of the overlap of the ages. Although Christ has been raised and his eschatological benefits have intruded into the present, believers still endure the present effects of sin. They have been saved definitively, but they await final and consummate deliverance when Christ returns. Believers have escaped corruption in the eschatological sense, but nevertheless experience it presently insofar as they experience the present age. If Peter's concern is to address eschatological deliverance, we must consider this partaking of the divine nature in conjunction with other passages that address liberation from corruption. Meredith Kline summarizes our concern well:

> In the vocabulary of Peter, "partakers of the divine nature" expresses renewal in the image of God (II Peter 1:4). In the context of this expression in II Peter 1, the figures of reflective transformation and of investiture are both found, the former with reference to the transfiguration of Jesus into the radiant likeness of the overshadowing Glory (vv. 16ff.) and the latter in reference to Peter's anticipated death, described as a divestiture, a negative counterpart to the resurrection investiture with glory (v. 14).[19]

Partaking of the divine nature means bearing the image of God, namely, in the consummated form of the resurrected Christ. It is a likeness to the divine original as well as a bestowal (or investiture) of divine glory. In salvation, believers escape the corruption in the world, which is a result of sin, by partaking of the likeness and benefits of the resurrected Christ. So we come to see how the eschatological progression of glory for the person

---

19. Kline, *Images of the Spirit*, 29.

of Christ has significance for the eschatological bestowal of that glory upon his people in redemptive history. But we should also note that this general head-image relationship is not exclusive to Christ and the age to come. A single representative, whose image is replicated among his progeny, characterizes both ages. After the fall, this worldly age is characterized by the first Adam, the disobedient son. The age to come is characterized by the last Adam, the obedient son. Each of these representatives embodies the wisdom or spirit of his particular age, and all men are found in one of the two Adams (Rom. 5:12–15; 1 Cor. 15:45). Through covenant identification and image conformity to the pattern of their federal head, each person acts according to the representative character of the age to which he belongs. According to Ephesians 1:3, the character of this union is personal, spiritual, and eschatological.[20] We may use this verse as a paradigm for understanding aspects of this two-age eschatology and its corresponding federal heads:

Characteristics of Union (Eph. 1:3)	This Age	Age to Come
Personal	First Adam	Last Adam, Jesus Christ
Spiritual	The spirit of this age	The Spirit of wisdom, the Holy Spirit
Eschatological	Hell	Heaven
Corresponding deeds	Disobedience	Obedience
Existence characterized by	Guilt/ corruption/death	Life

20. Lane G. Tipton, "Union with Christ: Its Foundational Status and Fundamental Structure (Part 1)," class lecture, Westminster Theological Seminary, March 12, 2010.

This overarching process of covenantal identity transfer and image conformity is fully Trinitarian. As believers are transferred from this age to the age to come, they are given a new life principle in the person of Christ. The Spirit enacts this union and enables believers to put this principle into action. This model elucidates Peter's eschatological conception behind the phrase "divine nature." To partake of the divine nature is to be identified with the ἔσχατος Ἀδὰμ (*eschatos Adam*), "the last Adam," having escaped this world's sinful corruption by being conformed to his image (Rom. 8:29) and ultimately resurrected in consummate glory (1 Cor. 15:20ff.).

A Reformed, Biblical-Theological Definition of Glorification

Having sketched an aeonic framework of image conformity as a biblical model for explicating God's gift of himself, we may now attempt a succinct definition of glorification. This subject warrants its own full-length study, but even an initial attempt will have value for addressing Rahner's proposal of ontological self-communication. The already/not-yet dimensions of glorification have not been fully explored by Reformed thinkers, and glorification is often considered entirely in terms of a future event. Indeed, significant elements of glorification remain unrealized—for example, further degrees of glory and bodily resurrection (1 Cor. 15:20ff.; 2 Cor. 3:18). At the same time, Paul often speaks about the present reality of the "new man" (Eph. 4:20–24). These aspects of glory are identified with the new creation (2 Cor. 5:17). The new creation is *yet* to come (Isa. 65:17ff.; 2 Peter 3:13; Rev. 21:1), but it has also *already* come. God's program of transformation is not entirely future. Those whom the Spirit has called, regenerated, and united to Christ experience the new man in the present time (Heb. 12:22). They have been made alive together with him and are seated in the heavenly places in Christ (Eph. 2:6). They rise to walk in newness of life (Rom. 6:4). Having died to sin, they have been and are being renewed (2 Cor. 4:16; Eph. 4:23; Col. 3:10). In a very real sense, believers already share in the glory of Christ and the hope of the glory to come, namely, that which is inextricably linked with Christ's return and the transformation that ensues as a necessary entailment of that event.[21] Still, the new man awaits a consummation. Believers do not yet outwardly manifest the glory that they will one day manifest when they see their Savior face to face. For at that time they will be changed in a moment, in the twinkling of an eye (1 Cor. 15:51–52).

The Reformed tradition's mild neglect of glorification as an overall program of image conformity becomes a pronounced challenge when Reformed theology is compared to Roman Catholicism, Eastern Orthodoxy, and the growing variety of deification and divinization theologies. On this score, Reformed thought is no more adequate than the others for addressing the particular challenges of Rahner's theology. The narrow view of glorification, which equates it with bodily resurrection, leaves open the opportunity to compromise the eschatological character of the salvific benefits. Within a comprehensive understanding of glorification as conformity to the image of the resurrected Christ, each distinct salvific benefit should be a component of this process, insofar as each salvific benefit is given for the purpose of making God's people more like Jesus Christ. For

---

21. Bodily resurrection still awaits the believer when Christ returns, not only to raise the bodies of the faithful, but also to raise the bodies of all people—both the just and the unjust (John 5:25; Acts 24:15). Of course, this general resurrection results in two very different modes of existence and eternal destinies. Believers are raised unto glory, receiving a σῶμα πνευματικόν (1 Cor. 15:44, *sōma pneumatikon*), which are bodies of the same harvest as that of the resurrected Christ (cf. 1 Cor. 15:20, 23). Unbelievers, however, are raised to a form of dishonor, being resurrected for judgment.

example, the Reformed tradition defines justification as the imputation of Christ's righteousness and the acquittal of sin's guilt. The Spirit imputes Christ's active and passive obedience to his people by grace alone through faith alone. And therefore, by justification, God's people share in Christ's righteousness, one facet of the glory of the resurrected Christ. Adoption and sanctification also contribute to moving believers from one degree of glory to another. In adoption, believers are received into the family of God and become heirs according to promise. Through sanctification, the power of sin is broken, and they are set apart as holy to the Lord. Throughout the rest of their earthly lives, the Spirit applies the death and resurrection of Christ to them, making them die increasingly to sin and raising them to newness of life. These distinct salvific benefits contribute in particular ways to reproducing the image of the resurrected Christ in each individual believer.

Justification, adoption, and sanctification—no less than glorification—are eschatological in character. The punishment for sin is death (physical and spiritual), and as long as believers are subject to physical death, they experience the effects of sin. The elect are already justified in this present age, but the outward manifestation of this acquittal from sin's guilt does not occur until the bodily resurrection. Only at the resurrection of the body does justification reach its open and public, future and eschatological, form (Rom. 8:1). Bodily resurrection marks the final and conclusive transition from this age to the age to come. This eschatological dynamic is true also with respect to adoption. Bodily resurrection also marks the revealing of the sons of glory and consummates adoption through the redemption of the body (Rom. 8:23). Furthermore, sanctification is completed when believers are finally redeemed. They are no longer subject to the struggles of the flesh and are finally and completely confirmed in righteousness. Each of these benefits brings increasing glory to God as his elect progressively take on the form of the man of heaven. They are being conformed to his image, reflecting his glory increasingly as the Spirit applies Christ's death and resurrection to them. Bodily resurrection is the premiere event of glorification; it is its capstone. Restricting this progress of glory to bodily resurrection, however, truncates the eschatological dimension of glory for each salvific benefit.

Therefore, by broadening the Reformed conception of glorification to include the not-yet aspects of justification, adoption, and sanctification, we seek to provide a Reformed, redemptive-historically nuanced (i.e., biblically and systematically informed) position. This will afford a true bestowal of Trinitarian glory that is neither possible on Rahner's own terms nor subject to their liabilities. Understood comprehensively, glorification is a complex of salvific events summarized as the redemptive-historical and progressive application to the elect of Christ's death and resurrection in all of its aspects, which culminates at the *parousia* in psychosomatic[22] resurrection and marks the terminal point of this age and the consummation of the age to come.

These concerns are bound up with our understanding of the image of God, how it changed after the fall, and how the Spirit restores and surpasses that original state in which man, as the image of God, was created. This image is renewed progressively and eschatologically in line with its threefold character. First, the functional glory increases as man increasingly fulfills his mandate on earth. Second, his ethical glory moves from a state of simple righteousness to one of confirmed righteousness.[23] Third, man's formal-physical glory advances as each believer receives a glorified body and moves from a σῶμα ψυχικόν (natural body, *sōma psychikon*) to a σῶμα πνευματικόν (spiritual

22. Here we intend to nuance the language of bodily resurrection to include not simply the physical body, but also the soul.

23. Kline, *Images of the Spirit*, 31.

body, *sōma pneumatikon*) (cf. 1 Cor. 15:44). This glorification of the individual recipients of saving grace follows the pattern of Christ's life, which exhibited a redemptive-historical progression from suffering to glory. Still, for Christ, archetypal experience is refracted by the reality of hypostatic union. As *Logos asarkos*, the eternal Son of God possesses eternal, infinite glory, though in his human nature even Christ progressed from one degree of glory to another. In terms of the formal-physical dimension of the image, he has moved from σῶμα ψυχικόν to σῶμα πνευματικόν (see 1 Cor. 15:44). Along the lines of the official dimension, Christ progressively exercised dominion over this aeon as he ministered and exercised his sovereignty through miracles— particularly over demonic forces operating according to the prince of the power of the air (see Eph. 2:2). His kingdom pro- gressively unfolded in power (see Luke 11:20). And in terms of the ethical dimension of the image, Christ grew in knowledge and stature in his human nature (Luke 2:52). His active obedi- ence likewise progressed toward consummation until he yielded his soul to death in his passive obedience (Ps. 31:5; Luke 23:46). Therefore, the threefold image of God was glorified eschatolog- ically in the human nature of Christ until that time when it was consummated in its fullness with the original glory that the Son possessed from all eternity.

In his high priestly prayer, Jesus asked the Father to glorify him "with the glory that I had with you before the world existed" (John 17:5). This request implied that he did not have this glory at the time of this prayer. The change of glory with respect to Christ's changing estates occurred for his human nature and must be understood in terms of the Chalcedonian Creed. At his resurrection, Christ was glorified in his human nature such that the original glory of the Trinity was revealed in a consum- mate, though ectypal, sense through his human nature. Christ exclaimed to Philip that if Philip had seen him, he had seen the

Father (John 14:9). This was so because the Son of God lives in a perichoretic relationship with both the Father and the Spirit from all eternity. To consider or see any one of the divine persons is to consider or see the Trinity. Surely, the persons of the Godhead are distinct, but they are also inseparable. Given this Trinitarian life, with respect to the person of Christ, his glory is original and unchanging. But with respect to Christ's human nature, his glory is derivative and eschatological.

The Christian life, then, analogously recapitulates this movement from one degree of glory to another (2 Cor. 3:18), circumscribed by the more basic and paradigmatic movement from suffering and humiliation to glory (Phil. 2:5–11). This relates directly to Christ's life and glory, but not identically or exhaustively. The image to which believers are conformed is an analogue or ectype of the heavenly archetype, which is the triune God perfectly imaged by Jesus Christ through hypostatic union (Col. 1:15). God's plan for the elect, then, is to move them from a position of protological and anticipatory glory to a position of eschatological and consummative glory by which they imitate the divine glory and reflect it climactically. In this model, the glory that believers exhibit in their resurrection is doubly derivative. It originates with the Godhead, is mediated through Christ's human nature, and then is displayed in glorified images of Christ. This eschatological program of image conformity climaxes in the beatific vision, which occurs at Christ's return, when his people see him and become like him (1 John 3:2). The triune God has always planned for the elect to move from one degree of glory to another, but after the fall into sin this program of image conformity took on a redemptive-historical and christocentric character. Rahner's conception of ontological self-communication is vastly different.

Glorification Distinguished from Ontological Self-Communication

Rahner's formulation of Trinitarian ontological self-communication runs directly counter to the preceding formulation of glorification as image-conformity. To rehearse our previous analysis briefly, Rahner refocused the theological discussion of this traditional theme by incorporating the scholastic concept of uncreated grace. Although Rahner maintains a place for both created and uncreated grace within his theology, his particular doctrinal concern centers on the latter, which for him is God's personal self-communication. God offers this gift to all human beings, and, by virtue of their constitution, they may freely accept this gift in transcendence. But not all reach for this gift. To guarantee the free offer, its free acceptance, and the subsequent elevation of human nature, Christ comes as *Realsymbol* through the hypostatic union.

The hypostatic union of the divine and human in the person of Jesus Christ is the pinnacle of history and metaphysics. Rahner formulates his particular doctrine of the hypostatic union in accord with his Ignatian and philosophical influences. He argues that the hypostatic union bears metaphysical significance for all humanity. The Son's incarnation incorporates all humanity into a new divine-human metaphysical relationship, because Christ becomes the new humanity. In effect, it forever and nearly universally links the transcendent and the immanent, Creator and creature. For Rahner, the beatific vision—the event and process of glorification—occurs through an ontological communication of God's person to the believer. While Rahner develops aspects of the beatific vision that are particular to Christ's personal human experience, the hypostatic union also bears salvific and metaphysical significance for humans universally. The bond between Christ and his people is ontological rather than spiritual, and therefore Rahner must also reject a covenantal view of union through which the elect are identified with Christ.

Rahner does speak of an "indwelling" of the Holy Spirit, when addressing the Trinitarian implications for grace.[24] But throughout his writings, the overwhelming emphasis is on Christ, and the personality of the Holy Spirit is underdeveloped. Christ, as the hypostatic union of divine and human natures, occupies a singular role in the gracious elevation of human beings. This is evident in Rahner's explanation of the beatific vision of Christ's human nature:

> Now it may and indeed must of course be said that the doctrine of the unconfused and unchanged real human nature implies, as the struggle against monothelitism after the rejection of monophysitism shows, that the "human nature" of the Logos possesses a genuine, spontaneous, free, spiritual, active centre, a human self-consciousness, which as creaturely faces the eternal Word in a genuinely human attitude of adoration, obedience, a most radical sense of creaturehood. Indeed it is emphatically maintained that this sphere of consciousness proper to a subject, a sphere enclosed in itself in creaturely fashion by reason of the gulf that distinguishes and separates God from the creature, only knows and only could know of its hypostatic union with the Logos in virtue of an objective communication. This communication is said to depend on the *visio beatifica* of this human consciousness, and cannot be a datum of Jesus' *human* self-consciousness—if by self-consciousness is understood the simple being-present-to-itself of an independent entity (in the identity of the act and object of knowledge). Thus by maintaining the genuineness of Christ's humanity, room is left within his life for achievement, and the possibility

24. Karl Rahner, *The Trinity* (New York: Crossroad, 1997), 34.

of a real Mediatorship and thus—if you will—of a real Messi-ahship is preserved.[25]

Christ is fully personal in his human nature, but this personality changes with respect to his self-consciousness when he receives the beatific vision. In that event he receives the divine gift of self and transcends his previous earthly existence. Christ's human consciousness recognizes that it is united hypostatically to the Logos only through an objective communication, which itself depends upon the beatific vision. But we may question where this leaves the Spirit, who has no corresponding created personal nature. Moreover, what becomes of the *personal* role of the Spirit in Christ's beatific vision, seeing that he receives the indwelling of the Holy Spirit himself? The hypostatic union complicates Christ's experience of the beatific vision, but Rahner does not develop the *personal* effects of spiritual indwelling for individual men and women either. It is not clear which person indwells: the Spirit or the Father. If the Father is the personal agent of *self*-communication, he must be identified more closely with the gift than the Son and Spirit. The Son and Spirit are means by which the Father's gift of self is given, and therefore ontological divine self-communication is not Trinitarian in content, but only in delivery.

Rahner is correct to insist that we receive God's grace through union and communion with him. However, he regrettably characterizes this gift as an original and immediate gift of essence. This gift of essential glory is always mediated through Christ's human nature. Rahner's protological impulse is sound, but his Scotist view of the incarnation is problematic. Christ came to this earth to save sinners, a distinctively *salvific* and

---

25. Karl Rahner, "Current Problems in Christology," in *Theological Investigations*, vol. 1, 2nd ed., trans. Cornelius Ernst (Baltimore: Helicon, 1965), 157–58.

redemptive purpose (see Mark 2:17; 10:45; 1 Tim. 1:15; Titus 2:14; Heb. 2:14, 16–17; 9:24–26). If the incarnation is then contingent upon the need for redemption, and the offer of eschatological glory is not, we must inquire how this glory would be bestowed if man had not sinned. In other words, we must elucidate the mode in which prelapsarian union and communion with the Trinitarian God is effected. Developing a response will further distinguish our view from Rahner's, because we must consider this union and communion in covenantal terms. The glory of the beatific vision is bestowed according to an image paradigm, and an image presupposes a relationship between that image and the original. This relationship between God and the recipients of saving grace should be understood covenantally, that is, as a bilateral and reciprocal bond of fellowship between God and his people. Rather than conceiving of this communion as an ontological gift of self, it should be seen as an eschatological perfection of human nature. It is eschatological, not essentially ethical.

This basic paradigm is in effect whether or not man falls into sin. In other words, glory-image conformity is not a postulate of soteriology.[26] If Adam had obeyed the terms of obedience in the garden, he would have been confirmed in knowledge, righteousness, and holiness. The Spirit would have elevated him to a consummate mode of existence according to a covenantally qualified image of the triune God. The original man would have entered into a higher form of communion with God. But when Adam disobeyed, redemption became necessary before consummation could be possible again. A new federal head was needed who would recover and consummate the covenantal glory held out to Adam from the very beginning. Only a divine-human

---

26. For a fuller treatment of the relationship of soteriology to protology and eschatology, see Gaffin, *Resurrection and Redemption*, 82n14.

being could do this: Jesus Christ, one person with divine and human natures. As God, he could succeed perfectly according to the terms of the covenant. As man, he could serve vicariously for his people. In contrast to Rahner's view, the mediation of hypostatic union would not be necessary prior to the fall into sin. This model arises more naturally from exegetical and biblical-theological reflection on Scripture.

If the biblical texts present a clear picture of eschatological transformation considered in light of a two-aeon federal eschatology, then Rahner's position is far from the mark. The preceding Reformed proposal of aeonic glory and kingdom identity, which derives from Christ's glory and identity as resurrected covenant Lord, differs from Rahner's conception of ontological self-communication through hypostatic union. The Holy Spirit indwells believers personally, yet the union that is established between believers and Christ is mystical, not hypostatic. Moreover, it accrues to God's people according to a covenantal arrangement, not through a substance metaphysic. The recipients of saving grace are conformed to the image of their new federal head, and the mode of image conformity is decidedly analogical or, better, *covenantal*.[27] Eternal, archetypal, Trinitarian glory cannot be communicated essentially and unequivocally to anything that has been created. The glory that Christ exhibits in his resurrection is Trinitarian in source and original with respect to his person, but ectypal as it is displayed throughout creation. Glorified saints participate in Christ's glory, but not essentially. Even before the fall into sin, God intended to perfect the Trinitarian glory-image in his people through the covenantal

---

27. Cornelius Van Til often spoke of human knowledge as *analogical* to God's knowledge. Whereas Van Til's teaching on the subject is insightful, the choice of language is less than helpful since it brings to mind the Thomist conceptions of analogy and other theological and philosophical schemes at odds with traditional Reformed theology.

communion bond. After the fall into sin, this original plan of glorification through image conformity required an additional step of redemption and covenantal transfer. Christ became the Redeemer and new federal head of his people by saving them from the consequences of the previously failed covenant arrangement and provided a new archetypal covenant image of glory. The Holy Spirit, who indwells believers, applies this image.

Conclusion

Rahner's desire to explicate the personal union and communion offered at creation and consummated in salvation is sound, but his theological formulations prevent him from explaining precisely how God gives the gift of *himself*. Rahner unwittingly concludes that divine self-communication is a partial gift that results in sub-Trinitarian union and communion. Thus, he does not deliver on his original promise. Notwithstanding, in Rahner's model, this partial gift effects entitative change, and therefore comes dangerously close to blurring the Creator-creature distinction. It remains to be seen how Rahner's conception of the hypostatic union, in its metaphysical significance for all believers, avoids committing this error. For the Son to assume human nature in general, and thereby incorporate each individual partaker of that nature, the hypostatic union (broadly considered) becomes a union of multiple personalities. Certainly the Son retains his unique personality, but Rahner also posits "hypostatic union" between the Son and each individual recipient of grace. If the hypostatic union found in the incarnation has *metaphysical* and *substantial* significance for all of humanity, there must be a plurality of persons united to the Son's divine nature. Since there is a genuine ontological (as opposed to mystical or covenantal) union of persons, this borders on an augmented form of Nestorianism.

Furthermore, if this gift is archetypal and results in an unmediated entitative change, we run increasingly counter to biblical teaching. Rahner's formulation lacks the theological category of "image" and "imitation," which protects against this danger (see Gen. 1:26–27; Rom. 8:29; 2 Cor. 3:18). In brief, Rahner's theology cannot sustain a fully Trinitarian self-communication. His errors result largely from a deficient methodological starting point of human experience and a deficient understanding of Trinitarian personality that subordinates the Son and Spirit to the Father. He makes the gift of divine self a patrimonic gift with no discernible metaphysical means for preventing an essential merger between God and humanity.

8

CONCLUSION

We have endeavored to offer a comprehensive study of Rahner's doctrine of Trinitarian personality. Having traced this thread through the doctrine of God, theological anthropology, Christology, and soteriology, we have been able to penetrate the deep structures of his thought. Whereas cursory studies inevitably caricature Rahner's Trinitarian axiom, we have allowed it to stand on its own terms. In so doing, we witnessed its collapse.

Rahner's notion of *perichoresis* begins with an unsatisfactory understanding of the *hypostases*, because it prioritized the unity of the Godhead over the diversity. He views the Father as the unoriginate *hypostasis* and the Son and Spirit as the twofold divine self-communication to humanity in categorical and transcendental experience. Man's twofold nature is expressed and mediated within a thoroughly personal atmosphere, which underscores all of God's interactions with humanity. Man is the spirit at the center of history, but that history is conditioned by God's free offer of himself in grace. Humans are specially created to receive this offer, and in freedom they may reach out to receive it. But even though he is there, they never fully reach God, who always remains an ineffable mystery. So the free subject reaches out to God more and more, but never fully arrives at the divine mystery. If God's self-communication is to be fully realized, Christ must come as the climactic divine gift of self equally matched by an irrevocable acceptance of that gift. Through the hypostatic union, Christ actualizes and consummates this relationship between God and man.

Rahner departed from the traditional view of the hypostatic union formulated at the Council of Chalcedon and defended by theologians such as Thomas Aquinas. The departure was due largely to methodological concerns. Rahner viewed Chalcedon as the beginning of an evolutionary development of doctrine. Accordingly, he drastically reconceived theology for a contemporary context by allowing his metaphysic to reinterpret Chalcedon. For Rahner, Christ became the new humanity and the *Realsymbol* of the divine self-communication to mankind. This was not something entirely new for Christ. The hypostatic union is a modal expression of the Son's eternal begottenness. When the eternal Son of God expresses himself concretely, he does so as a hypostatic union of divine and human natures. The concrete actualization of the Son's distinctive mode of subsistence guarantees the perfect union of divine self-giving and the human acceptance of that gift in freedom. Christ's specific hypostatic union becomes an archetype for the ontological union that is repeated in each individual's experience of salvation in history. Whenever individual human beings reach out toward the divine mystery and accept the free offer of self, they experience ectypal hypostatic union. This gift and its reception are thoroughly personal—characterized by thought, emotion, and freedom—and human persons enter into a heightened relationship with the divine persons. The reception of this divine gift of self elevates humanity to a consummated life through the beatific vision.

Although Rahner wanted to maintain this personal gift

through the Son and the Spirit, his Trinitarian theology could not support it. His formulation of *perichoresis* stops short of exhaustive hypostatic penetration *within* the divine essence. Without understanding rightly the eternal ontic status of Father, Son, and Spirit, Rahner could not formulate a doctrine to describe how they mutually coinhere. He was forced to choose between personal unity and personal diversity, driving his view toward panentheism or forms of Monarchianism. The Father, as the unoriginate *hypostasis*, self-communicates via the Son and Spirit. But since Son and Spirit do not exhibit fully the absolute personality ascribed to the Father, the Father's self-communication is uni-personal and patrimonic.

By appealing to the twentieth-century Reformed theologian Cornelius Van Til, we proposed a fuller understanding of *perichoresis*, in which God exists simultaneously and exhaustively in his unity and as three persons, as true, absolute, triune personality. Rahner's Eastern doctrine of the Trinity and Trinitarian personality precludes him from incorporating this proposal. In starting from the priority of the Father and then the human experience of the Son and Spirit, Rahner eliminated any possibility of a truly Trinitarian self-communication to humanity. Problems multiply when this truncated self-communication is characterized as a divine ontological self-communication. Rahner's theological and metaphysical framework does not have any means of protecting the Creator-creature distinction, and though Rahner rejected the notion that God and humanity merge substantially, he failed to offer any response beyond an assertion.

We sketched a model of aeonic image conformity as a biblical-theological and systematic alternative. The beatific vision (and glorification) ought to be construed in a covenantal context as an eschatological transformation, which recovers the three-fold image of God bestowed upon man at creation and elevates him to an estate higher than that in which he was created. In contrast to Rahner's theology of divine self-communication, the glorified man does not become incorporated ontologically or hypostatically into God. As believers are conformed to the image of Christ, they participate in his resurrection glory, manifesting more fully the resurrection glory's ultimate source, God himself.

Prospect

Rahner remains widely influential in Catholic theology and a perennial dialogue partner in mainline Protestant thought. But he has gone virtually unnoticed in the confessionally Reformed church. Reformed theologians will have fundamental differences with Rahner regarding nearly all theological *loci*. Nevertheless, Rahner asked many important theological questions that deserve confessionally Reformed attention. Too easily, critics dismiss those who are most different from themselves without doing the homework of truly understanding them. We would be better served by studying Rahner on his own terms. Only then can we understand his theological formulations and see their value for ecumenical dialogue—not for the purpose of superficial rapprochement, but for sharpening our understanding of God's desire to bring his people into consummated union and communion with him.

GLOSSARY

.

economic Trinity. The Trinity in relation to creation. Although it is a great mystery, in God's eternal decree, the Father, Son, and Holy Spirit adopt particular roles in creating and then consummating that creation. With regard to redemption, these include the Father electing a people to save, the Son becoming incarnate to live, die, and be raised for their salvation, and the Spirit applying the benefits of Christ to the elect.

immanent Trinity. The Trinity as each member relates to the others. The term refers to the persons as they indwell one another, subsisting in the divine essence. This term is distinct from *imminent*, which refers to an event being temporally proximate or ready to happen. Many in the Reformed tradition use the term *ontological* instead of *immanent* to emphasize the being of God *in se* (in itself).

magisterium. The teaching authority of the Roman Catholic Church. In Catholic belief, God has granted to the Church the authority and ability to interpret the Word of God correctly. The *Catechism of the Catholic Church* affirms, "The task of interpreting the Word of God authentically has been entrusted solely to the Magisterium of the Church, that is, to the Pope and to the bishops in communion with him" (*Catechism of the Catholic Church*, paragraph 100).

ontological. Concerned with being or existence. This word derives from *ontology*, which is the philosophical study of being. Some philosophers, such as Martin Heidegger, distinguish between *ontological* and *ontic*. The latter refers to the character of a thing as it exists; the former refers to the study of such being. The term *ontological Trinity* is often used in Protestant theology to refer to the Trinity *in se* (in itself) and apart from creation, that is, without economic considerations.

Second Vatican Council. A council of the Roman Catholic Church called to address the Church's relationship to the modern world. The council was called by Pope John XXIII and began on October 11, 1962; it concluded under Pope Paul VI on December 8, 1965.

Trinitarian missions. The economic roles and respective purposes of the Father, Son, and Holy Spirit. These are the temporal processions of the persons. The Father "sent" his Son (John 7:28; Gal. 4:4). He also "sent" the Spirit (Gal. 4:6).

Trinitarian processions. The manner in which each person of the Trinity subsists in the divine essence. In the Latin (Western) church tradition, the Father is unbegotten, the Son is begotten, and the Spirit proceeds from the Father and the Son. There was a great schism between the Greek (Eastern) and Latin (Western) branches of the church in 1054 over the nature of the Spirit's procession. The East denies that the Spirit proceeds from the Son.

INTRODUCTORY WORKS
ON KARL RAHNER

Dych, William V. *Karl Rahner*. Collegeville MN: Liturgical Press, 1992.

Egan, Harvey. *Karl Rahner: Mystic of Everyday Life*. New York: Crossroad, 1998.

Kilby, Karen. *Karl Rahner: A Brief Introduction*. New York: Crossroad, 2007.

Vorgrimler, Herbert. *Understanding Karl Rahner: An Introduction to His Life and Thought*. New York: Crossroad, 1986.

A Plan for Reading Rahner

Rahner is difficult to access, in part because he wrote so much. His *curriculum vitae* contains more than 4,000 items. I suggest beginning with Rahner's *Foundations of Christian Faith*. I would also begin reading a few of his articles, which may be found in his series *Theological Investigations* (*TI* for short). In my judgment, the most foundational articles are:

- "Christology within an Evolutionary View of the World" (*TI* 5:157–92)
- "The Concept of Mystery in Catholic Theology" (*TI* 4:36–73)
- "The Two Basic Types of Christology" (*TI* 13:213–23)
- "Some Implications of the Scholastic Concept of Uncreated Grace" (*TI* 1:319–46)

For more advanced study, I suggest turning to Rahner's books *Hearers of the Word* and *Spirit in the World*. Do not become discouraged if Rahner seems inaccessible. I trust that with the help of the present study and the willingness to "sit" with Rahner for an extended period of time, the patient reader will grasp not only the basic contours of his thought, but also its foundations.

BIBLIOGRAPHY

Adam, Karl. *The Christ of Faith: The Christology of the Church.* London: Burns & Oates, 1957.

Alberigo, Giuseppe, and Joseph A. Komonchak. *History of Vatican II.* Maryknoll, NY: Orbis Books; Leuven: Peeters, 1995.

Anselm. *Proslogium; Monologium; an Appendix, In Behalf of the Fool, by Gaunilon; and Cur Deus Homo.* Reprint ed. Philosophical Classics: Religion of Science Library, no. 54. Chicago: Open Court Pub. Co., 1939.

Backes, Ignaz. *Die Christologie des hl. Thomas v. Aquin und die griechischen Kirchenväter.* Paderborn: Schöningh, 1931.

Bahnsen, Greg L. *Presuppositional Apologetics: Stated and Defended.* Powder Springs, GA: American Vision Inc./Nacogdoches, TX: Covenant Media Press, 2008.

―――. *Van Til's Apologetic: Readings and Analysis.* Phillipsburg, NJ: P&R Publishing, 1998.

Barnett, Paul. *The Message of 2 Corinthians: Power in Weakness.* Downers Grove, IL: InterVarsity Press, 1988.

Barth, Karl. *Church Dogmatics.* Vol. I.1, *The Doctrine of the Word of*

God. Edited by G. W. Bromiley and T. F. Torrance. Peabody, MA: Hendrickson Publishers, 2010.

———. *Church Dogmatics*. Vol. II, *The Doctrine of God*. Edited by G. W. Bromiley and T. F. Torrance. Peabody, MA: Hendrickson Publishers, 2010.

———. *Church Dogmatics*. Vol. IV.1, *The Doctrine of Reconciliation*. Edited by G. W. Bromiley and T. F. Torrance. Peabody, MA: Hendrickson Publishers, 2010.

Batlogg, Andreas R., Melvin E. Michalski, and Barbara G. Turner, eds. *Encounters with Karl Rahner: Remembrances of Rahner by Those Who Knew Him*. Milwaukee: Marquette University Press, 2009.

Bavinck, Herman. *Reformed Dogmatics*. Vol. 2, *God and Creation*. Edited by John Bolt. Translated by John Vriend. Grand Rapids: Baker Academic, 2004.

———. *Reformed Dogmatics*. Vol. 3, *Sin and Salvation in Christ*. Grand Rapids: Baker Academic, 2006.

Bergin, Liam. *O Propheticum Lavacrum: Baptism as Symbolic Act of Eschatological Salvation*. Rome: Editrice Pontifica Università Gregoriana, 1999.

Berkhof, Louis. *Systematic Theology*. Grand Rapids: Eerdmans, 1996.

Berkouwer, G. C. *The Return of Christ*. Grand Rapids: Eerdmans, 1972.

Billings, J. Todd. *Calvin, Participation, and the Gift: The Activity of Believers in Union with Christ*. Changing Paradigms in Historical and Systematic Theology. Oxford/New York: Oxford University Press, 2007.

Blackwell, Ben C. *Christosis: Pauline Soteriology in Light of Deification in Irenaeus and Cyril of Alexandria*. Wissenschaftliche Untersuchungen zum Neuen Testament 2/314. Tübingen: Mohr Siebeck, 2011.

Bray, Gerald. *The Doctrine of God*. Contours of Christian Theology. Downers Grove, IL: InterVarsity Press, 1993.

Brezik, Victor B., ed. *One Hundred Years of Thomism: Aeterni Patris and Afterwards, A Symposium*. Houston: Center for Thomistic Studies, University of St. Thomas, 1981.

Bromiley, Geoffrey William. *Introduction to the Theology of Karl Barth*. Edinburgh: T&T Clark, 2001.

Brown, Robert McAfee. *Observer in Rome: A Protestant Report on the Vatican Council*. Garden City, NY: Doubleday, 1964.

Burke, Patrick. *Reinterpreting Rahner*. New York: Fordham University Press, 2002.

Burrell, David. *Aquinas: God and Action*. Notre Dame, IN: University of Notre Dame Press, 1979.

Butler, Christopher. *The Theology of Vatican II*. London: Darton, Longman & Todd, 1967.

Calvin, Jean. *The Epistles of Paul the Apostle to the Romans and to the Thessalonians*. Grand Rapids: Eerdmans, 1960.

Candelario, Ma. Delia A. "George Tyrrell and Karl Rahner: A Dialogue on Revelation." *Heythrop Journal* 50, no. 1 (January 1, 2009): 44–57.

Canlis, Julie. *Calvin's Ladder: A Spiritual Theology of Ascent and Ascension*. Grand Rapids: Eerdmans, 2010.

Caponi, Francis J. "Karl Rahner: Divinization in Roman Catholicism." In *Partakers of the Divine Nature: The History and Development of Deification in the Christian Traditions*, edited by Michael J. Christensen and Jeffery A. Wittung, 259–80. Grand Rapids: Baker Academic, 2008.

Chenu, Marie-Dominique. *Toward Understanding Saint Thomas*. Chicago: Regnery, 1964.

Chiavone, M. L. "The Unity of God as Understood by Four Twentieth Century Trinitarian Theologians: Karl Rahner, Millard Erickson, John Zizioulas, and Wolfhart Pannenberg." PhD diss., Southeastern Baptist Theological Seminary, 2005.

Christensen, Michael J., and Jeffery A. Wittung, eds. *Partakers of the Divine Nature: The History and Development of Deification in the Christian Traditions*. Grand Rapids: Baker Academic, 2008.

Clark, R. Scott, ed. *Covenant, Justification, and Pastoral Ministry: Essays by the Faculty of Westminster Seminary California*. Phillipsburg, NJ: P&R Publishing, 2007.

Clifford, Anne. *Christology: Memory, Inquiry, Practice*. Maryknoll, NY: Orbis Books, 2003.

Daly, Gabriel. *Transcendence and Immanence: A Study in Catholic Modernism and Integralism*. Oxford: Clarendon Press, 1980.

De Chirico, Leonardo. "Evangelical Theological Perspectives on Post-Vatican II Roman Catholicism." PhD thesis, University of London, 2003.

Dempsey, Michael T. *Trinity and Election in Contemporary Theology*. Grand Rapids: Eerdmans, 2011.

Denzinger, Heinrich. *The Sources of Catholic Dogma*. Translated by Roy J. Deferrari. St. Louis: B. Herder Book Co., 1957.

Denzinger, Henrico, and Clemens Bannwart. *Enchiridion Symbolorum, Definitionum et Declarationum de Rebus Fidei et Morum*. Friburgi Brisgoviae: Herder, 1908.

DiNoia, Joseph A. "Nature, Grace, and Experience: Karl Rahner's Theology of Human Transformation." *Philosophy & Theology* 7, no. 2 (December 1, 1992): 115–26.

Dolezal, James E. "Trinity, Simplicity and the Status of God's Personal Relations." *International Journal of Systematic Theology* (2013). https://doi.org/10.1111/ijst.12016.

Donohue-White, Patricia, Stephen J. Grabill, Christopher Westley, and Gloria Zúñiga. *Human Nature and the Discipline of Economics: Personalist Anthropology and Economic Methodology*. Lanham, MD: Lexington Books, 2002.

Donovan, Daniel. "Revelation and Faith." In *The Cambridge Companion to Karl Rahner*, edited by Declan Marmion and

Mary E. Hines, 83–97. Cambridge: Cambridge University Press, 2005.

Dych, Willifam V. *Karl Rahner*. Collegeville, MN: Liturgical Press, 1992.

———. "Method in Theology according to Karl Rahner." In *Theology and Discovery: Essays in Honor of Karl Rahner, S.J.*, edited by William J. Kelly, 39–53. Milwaukee: Marquette University Press, 1980.

Egan, Harvey. *Karl Rahner: Mystic of Everyday Life*. New York: Crossroad, 1998.

———. "Rahner's Mystical Theology." In *Theology and Discovery: Essays in Honor of Karl Rahner, S.J.*, edited by William J. Kelly, 139–58. Milwaukee: Marquette University Press, 1980.

Emery, Gilles, and Francesca Aran Murphy. *The Trinitarian Theology of Saint Thomas Aquinas*. Oxford: Oxford University Press, 2010.

Endean, Philip. "Has Rahnerian Theology a Future?" In *The Cambridge Companion to Karl Rahner*, edited by Declan Marmion and Mary E. Hines, 281–96. Cambridge: Cambridge University Press, 2005.

———. *Karl Rahner and Ignatian Spirituality*. Oxford: Oxford University Press, 2001.

———. "Rahner, Christology and Grace." *Heythrop Journal* 37, no. 3 (1996): 284–97.

Erickson, Millard J. *Christian Theology*. 3rd ed. Grand Rapids: Baker Book House, 2013.

Evans, William B. *Imputation and Impartation: Union with Christ in American Reformed Theology*. Eugene, OR: Wipf & Stock, 2009.

Fahlbusch, Erwin, Jan Milič Lochman, John Mbiti, Jaroslav Pelikan, and Lukas Vischer, eds. *The Encyclopedia of Christianity*. Translated by Geoffrey W. Bromiley. 5 vols. Grand Rapids: Eerdmans, 1999–2008.

Fields, Stephen. "Balthasar and Rahner on the Spiritual Senses." *Theological Studies* 57 (1996): 224–41.

———. *Being as Symbol: On the Origins and Development of Karl Rahner's Metaphysics*. Washington: Georgetown University Press, 2000.

Fischer, Mark F. *The Foundations of Karl Rahner: A Paraphrase of the Foundations of Christian Faith, with Introduction and Indices*. New York: Crossroad, 2005.

Ford, David F., and Rachel Muers, eds. *The Modern Theologians: An Introduction to Christian Theology since 1918*. 3rd ed. Malden, MA: Blackwell, 2005.

Fritz, Peter Joseph. *Karl Rahner's Theological Aesthetics*. Washington: Catholic University of America Press, 2014.

Gächter, P. "Zum Pneumabegriff des heiligen Paulus." *Zeitschrift für Katholische Theologie* 53 (1929): 345–408.

Gaffin, Richard B., Jr. *By Faith Not by Sight: Paul and the Order of Salvation*. Milton Keynes: Paternoster, 2006.

———. "'Life-Giving Spirit': Probing the Center of Paul's Pneumatology." *Journal of the Evangelical Theological Society* 41 (1998): 573–89.

———. *Resurrection and Redemption: A Study in Paul's Soteriology*. 2nd ed. Phillipsburg, NJ: Presbyterian and Reformed, 1987.

Galvin, John P. "The Invitation of Grace." In *A World of Grace: An Introduction to the Themes and Foundations of Karl Rahner's Theology*, 64–75. Washington: Georgetown University Press, 1995.

———. "Theology of Karl Rahner." Catholic University of America, Washington, DC, January 12, 2011.

Garcia, Mark A. *Life in Christ: Union with Christ and Twofold Grace in Calvin's Theology*. Studies in Christian History and Thought. Milton Keynes, UK/Colorado Springs, CO: Paternoster, 2008.

Garner, David B. "Adoption in Christ." PhD diss., Westminster Theological Seminary, 2002.

Geenen, G. "En marge du Concile de Chalcédoine. Les textes du Quatrième Concile dans les oeuvres de Saint Thomas." *Angelicum* 29 (1952): 43–59.

Gerhart, Mary. *Metaphoric Process: The Creation of Scientific and Religious Understanding.* Fort Worth: Texas Christian University Press, 1984.

———. *New Maps for Old: Explorations in Science and Religion.* New York: Continuum, 2001.

Gondreau, Paul. "The Humanity of Christ, the Incarnate Word." In *The Theology of Thomas Aquinas*, edited by Rik van Nieuwenhove and Joseph Wawrykow, 252–76. Notre Dame, IN: University of Notre Dame Press, 2005.

Grenz, Stanley J. *Rediscovering the Triune God: The Trinity in Contemporary Theology.* Minneapolis: Fortress, 2004.

———. *The Social God and the Relational Self: A Trinitarian Theology of the Imago Dei.* Louisville, KY: Westminster John Knox, 2001.

Grudem, Wayne. *Systematic Theology: An Introduction to Biblical Doctrine.* Leicester: Inter-Varsity Press/Grand Rapids: Zondervan, 2000.

Harrower, Scott D. *Trinitarian Self and Salvation: An Evangelical Engagement with Rahner's Rule.* Eugene, OR: Pickwick Publications, 2012.

Hart, D. G. "Beyond the Battle for the Bible: What Evangelicals Missed in Van Til's Critique of Barth." In *Karl Barth and American Evangelicalism*, edited by Bruce L. McCormack and Clifford B. Anderson, 42–70. Grand Rapids: Eerdmans, 2011.

Henle, Robert J. "Transcendental Thomism: A Critical Assessment." In *One Hundred Years of Thomism: Aeterni Patris and Afterwards, A Symposium*, edited by Victor B. Brezik,

90–116. Houston: Center for Thomistic Studies, University of St. Thomas, 1981.

Hennesey, James. "Leo XIII's Thomistic Revival: A Political and Philosophical Event." *Journal of Religion* 58, Supplement (1978): 185–97.

Hill, William J. *The Three-Personed God: The Trinity as a Mystery of Salvation.* Washington: Catholic University of America Press, 1982.

Hodge, Charles. *Systematic Theology.* 3 vols. Peabody, MA: Hendrickson, 1999.

Hoeksema, Herman. *Reformed Dogmatics.* Grand Rapids: Reformed Free Publishing Association, 1985.

Horton, Douglas. *Vatican Diary, 1963: A Protestant Observes the Second Session of Vatican Council II.* Philadelphia: United Church Press, 1964.

Horton, Michael. *The Christian Faith: A Systematic Theology for Pilgrims on the Way.* Grand Rapids: Zondervan, 2011.

———. *Covenant and Salvation: Union with Christ.* Louisville: Westminster John Knox, 2007.

Hughes, Christopher. *On a Complex Theory of a Simple God: An Investigation in Aquinas' Philosophical Theology.* Ithaca: Cornell University Press, 1989.

Hunsinger, George. *Disruptive Grace: Studies in the Theology of Karl Barth.* Grand Rapids: Eerdmans, 2000.

———. *How to Read Karl Barth: The Shape of His Theology.* New York: Oxford University Press, 1991.

Jodock, Darrell, ed. *Catholicism Contending with Modernity: Roman Catholic Modernism and Anti-Modernism in Historical Context.* Cambridge: Cambridge University Press, 2000.

Jones, Gareth. *The Blackwell Companion to Modern Theology.* Malden, MA: Blackwell, 2004.

Jordan, Mark D. *Rewritten Theology: Aquinas after His Readers.* Malden, MA/Oxford: Blackwell, 2006.

Kamesar, Adam. "The *Logos Endiathetos* and the *Logos Prophorikos* in Allegorical Interpretation: Philo and the D-Scholia to the *Iliad*." *Greek, Roman, and Byzantine Studies* 44 (2004): 163–81.

"Karen Kilby—The University of Nottingham." Accessed January 8, 2011. http://www.nottingham.ac.uk/theology/people/karen.kilby.

Kärkkäinen, Veli-Matti. *The Trinity: Global Perspectives.* Louisville, KY: Westminster John Knox, 2007.

Kelly, J. N. D. *Early Christian Doctrines.* San Francisco: HarperSanFrancisco, 1978.

Kerr, Fergus. *After Aquinas: Versions of Thomism.* Malden, MA: Blackwell, 2002.

———. *Twentieth-Century Catholic Theologians: From Neoscholasticism to Nuptial Mysticism.* Malden, MA: Blackwell, 2007.

Kilby, Karen. *Karl Rahner: A Brief Introduction.* New York: Crossroad, 2007.

———. *Karl Rahner: Theology and Philosophy.* London, New York: Routledge, 2004.

———. "Philosophy, Theology and Foundationalism in the Thought of Karl Rahner." *Scottish Journal of Theology* 55, no. 2 (May 1, 2002): 127–40.

———. "Rahner." In *The Blackwell Companion to Modern Theology*, edited by Gareth Jones, 343–56. Malden, MA: Blackwell, 2004.

———. "The *Vorgriff auf Esse*: A Study in the Relation of Philosophy to Theology in the Thought of Karl Rahner." PhD diss., Yale University, 1994.

Kline, Meredith G. *God, Heaven, and Har Magedon: A Covenantal Tale of Cosmos and Telos.* Eugene, OR: Wipf & Stock, 2006.

———. *Images of the Spirit.* Eugene, OR: Wipf and Stock, 1999.

Klinger, Elmar, Karl Rahner, and Klaus Wittstadt. *Glaube im Prozess: Christsein nach dem II. Vatikanum: für Karl Rahner*. Freiburg im Breisgau: Herder, 1984.

Knasas, John F. X. *Being and Some Twentieth-Century Thomists*. New York: Fordham University Press, 2003.

———. "*Esse* as the Target of Judgment in Rahner and Aquinas." *The Thomist* 51 (1987): 222–45.

Küng, Hans. *My Struggle for Freedom: Memoirs*. Translated by John Bowden. Grand Rapids: Eerdmans, 2003.

Kurtz, Lester R. *The Politics of Heresy: The Modernist Crisis in Roman Catholicism*. Berkeley: University of California Press, 1986.

LaCugna, Catherine Mowry. *God for Us: The Trinity and Christian Life*. San Francisco: HarperSanFrancisco, 1991.

———. "Introduction." In *The Trinity*, by Karl Rahner, vii–xxi. New York: Crossroad, 1997.

Lamb, Matthew, and Matthew Levering, eds. *Vatican II: Renewal within Tradition*. Oxford: Oxford University Press, 2008.

Letham, Robert. *The Holy Trinity: In Scripture, History, Theology, and Worship*. Phillipsburg, NJ: P&R Publishing, 2005.

Leo XIII. *Aeterni Patris: Encyclical of Pope Leo XIII on the Restoration of Christian Philosophy*, 1879. Accessed May 7, 2012. http://www.vatican.va/holy_father/leo_xiii/encyclicals/documents/hf_l-xiii_enc_04081879_aeterni-patris_en.html.

Lillback, Peter. *The Binding of God: Calvin's Role in the Development of Covenant Theology*. Grand Rapids: Baker Academic/Carlisle: Paternoster, 2001.

Lillback, Peter, and D. Claire Davis, eds. *The Practical Calvinist: An Introduction the Presbyterian and Reformed Heritage*. Fearn, UK: Mentor, 2003.

Lindbeck, George. *The Nature of Doctrine: Religion and Theology in a Postliberal Age*. Philadelphia: Westminster, 1984.

Livingston, James C., Francis Schüssler Fiorenza, Sarah Coakley, and James H. Evans Jr. *Modern Christian Thought: The Twentieth Century*. 2nd ed. Minneapolis: Fortress, 2006.

Lubac, Henri de. *The Mystery of the Supernatural*. New York: Herder and Herder, 1967.

Maréchal, Joseph. *A Maréchal Reader*. Edited and translated by Joseph Donceel. New York: Herder and Herder, 1970.

Marmion, Declan. "Rahner and His Critics: Revisiting the Dialogue." *Irish Theological Quarterly* 68, no. 3 (September 1, 2003): 195–212.

———. *A Spirituality of Everyday Faith: A Theological Investigation of the Notion of Spirituality in Karl Rahner*. Louvain: Peeters, 1998.

Marmion, Declan, and Mary E. Hines. *The Cambridge Companion to Karl Rahner*. Cambridge Companions to Religion. Cambridge: Cambridge University Press, 2005.

Marmion, Declan, and Rik van Nieuwenhove. *An Introduction to the Trinity*. Cambridge: Cambridge University Press, 2010.

Martin, Ralph. *2 Corinthians*. Word Biblical Commentary 40. Waco, TX: Word Books, 1986.

Masson, Robert. "Analogy and Metaphoric Process." *Theological Studies* 62, no. 3 (2001): 571–96.

———. "The Class of Christological Symbols: A Case for Metaphoric Realism." In *Christology: Memory, Inquiry, Practice*, edited by Anne M. Clifford and Anthony J. Godzieba, 62–86. Maryknoll, NY: Orbis, 2003.

———. "The Force of Analogy." *Anglican Theological Review* 87, no. 3 (2005): 471–86.

———. "Interpreting Rahner's Metaphoric Logic." *Theological Studies* 71, no. 2 (2010): 380–409.

———. "Rahner and Heidegger: Being, Hearing, and God." *The Thomist* 37 (1973): 455–88.

————. "Rahner's Primordial Words and Bernstein's Metaphorical Leaps: The Affinity of Art with Religion and Theology." *Horizons* 33, no. 2 (2006): 276–97.

————. "Reframing the Fields." *Zygon* 39, no. 1 (March 1, 2004): 49–62.

————. Review of *Karl Rahner: Theology and Philosophy*, by Karen Kilby. *Modern Theology* 23, no. 1 (January 1, 2007): 157–60.

————. "Saving God." *Horizons* 31, no. 2 (2004): 239–71.

McCool, Gerald A. *Catholic Theology in the Nineteenth Century: The Quest for a Unitary Method*. New York: Seabury, 1977.

————. "Karl Rahner and the Christian Philosophy of St. Thomas Aquinas." In *Theology and Discovery: Essays in Honor of Karl Rahner, S.J.*, edited by William J. Kelly, 63–93. Milwaukee: Marquette University Press, 1980.

McCormack, Bruce L. "Grace and Being: The Role of God's Gracious Election in Karl Barth's Theological Ontology." In *Orthodox and Modern: Studies in the Theology of Karl Barth*, 183–200. Grand Rapids: Baker Academic, 2008.

Molnar, Paul. "Can We Know God Directly? Rahner's Solution from Experience." *Theological Studies* 46, no. 1 (1985): 228–61.

————. *Divine Freedom and the Doctrine of the Immanent Trinity: In Dialogue with Karl Barth and Contemporary Theology*. London, New York: T&T Clark, 2002.

Moltmann, Jürgen. *The Trinity and the Kingdom: The Doctrine of God*. Minneapolis: Fortress, 1993.

Morard, Martin. "Une source de Saint Thomas d'Aquin: Le deuxième Concile de Constantinople (553)." *Revue des Sciences Philosophiques et Théologiques* 81, no. 1 (1997): 21–56.

Mosser, Carl. "The Greatest Possible Blessing: Calvin and Deification." *Scottish Journal of Theology* 55, no. 1 (February 1, 2002): 36–57.

Muck, Otto. *The Transcendental Method*. New York: Herder and Herder, 1968.

Muller, Richard A. *Post-Reformation Reformed Dogmatics: The Rise and Development of Reformed Orthodoxy*, ca. 1520 to ca. 1725. 2nd ed. Grand Rapids: Baker Academic, 2003.

Murray, John. *The Imputation of Adam's Sin*. Grand Rapids: Eerdmans, 1959.

Nazianzus, Gregory. "Oration 40, The Oration on Holy Baptism." New Advent. Accessed June 7, 2019. http://www.new advent.org/fathers/310240.htm.

Neufeld, Karl H. *Die Brüder Rahner: Eine Biographie*. Freiburg: Herder, 1994.

O'Connell, Marvin Richard. *Critics on Trial: An Introduction to the Catholic Modernist Crisis*. Washington: Catholic University of America Press, 1994.

O'Donnell, John J. *Karl Rahner: Life in the Spirit*. Rome: Gregorian University Press, 2004.

O'Donovan, Leo J. "Karl Rahner, SJ (1904–84): A Theologian for the Twenty-First Century." *Theology Today* 62, no. 3 (2005): 352–63.

O'Donovan, Leo J., ed. *A World of Grace: An Introduction to the Themes and Foundations of Karl Rahner's Theology*. Washington: Georgetown University Press, 1995.

O'Malley, John. *What Happened at Vatican II*. Cambridge, MA: Belknap, 2008.

Oliphint, K. Scott. *Justified in Christ: God's Plan for Us in Justification*. Fearn, UK: Mentor, 2007.

———. *Reasons for Faith: Philosophy in the Service of Theology*. Phillipsburg, NJ: P&R Publishing, 2006.

Olson, Roger E., and Christopher Alan Hall. *The Trinity*. Guides to Theology. Grand Rapids: Eerdmans, 2002.

Ormerod, N. "Two Points or Four—Rahner and Lonergan on

Trinity, Incarnation, Grace, and Beatific Vision." *Theological Studies* 68, no. 3 (2007): 661–73.

Palmer, Edwin. *Scheeben's Doctrine of Divine Adoption*. Kampen: J. H. Kok, 1953.

Pannenberg, Wolfhart. "The Christian Vision of God: The New Discussion on the Trinitarian Doctrine." *Asbury Theological Journal* 46, no. 2 (Fall 1991): 27–36.

———. *Systematic Theology*. Vol. 1. Translated by Geoffrey W. Bromiley. Grand Rapids: Eerdmans, 1991.

Pasnau, Robert. *Theories of Cognition in the Later Middle Ages*. Cambridge/New York: Cambridge University Press, 1997.

Perkins, William. *A Golden Chain: or, The Description of Theology Containing the Order of the Causes of Salvation and Damnation, according to God's Word*. Puritan Reprints. Port St. Lucie, FL: Solid Ground Christian Books, 2010.

Peters, Ted. *God as Trinity: Relationality and Temporality in Divine Life*. Louisville, KY: Westminster / John Knox, 1993.

———. *God—the World's Future: Systematic Theology for a New Era*. Minneapolis: Fortress, 2000.

Phillips, Winfred George. "Rahner's Transcendental Deduction of the *Vorgriff*." *The Thomist* 56 (1992): 257–90.

Piderit, John J., and Melanie M. Morey. *Teaching the Tradition: Catholic Themes in Academic Disciplines*. New York: Oxford University Press, 2012.

Pius X. "The Oath against Modernism," 1910. Accessed June 7, 2019. http://www.papalencyclicals.net/Pius10/p10moath .htm.

Pojman, Louis. *The Theory of Knowledge: Classical and Contemporary Readings*. 3rd ed. Belmont, CA: Wadsworth, 2003.

Poythress, Vern S. "Structural Approaches to Understanding the Theology of the Apostle Paul." DTh thesis, University of Stellenbosch, 1981.

———. *Using Multiple Thematic Centers in Theological Synthesis:*

Holiness as a Test Case in Developing a Pauline Theology.
Glenside, PA: Westminster Theological Seminary, 1991.

Raffelt, Albert. "Bibliographie Karl Rahner." Universitätsbiblio-
thek Freiburg im Breisgau, 2013. Accessed December 3,
2013. http://www.ub.uni-freiburg.de/fileadmin/ub/referate
/04/rahner/rahnersc.pdf.

Rahner, Karl. *Bekenntnisse: Rückblick auf 80 Jahre*. Edited by
Georg Sporschill. Wien, München: Herold, 1984.

———. "Brief Observations on Systematic Christology Today."
In *Theological Investigations* 21:233–34, translated by Hugh
M. Riley. London: Darton, Longman & Todd, 1988.

———. *Christian at the Crossroads*. Translated by V. Green. New
York: Seabury, 1975.

———. "Die Christologie innerhalb evolutiver Weltanschauung."
In *Sämtliche Werke*, vol. 15, *Verantwortung der Theologie*,
edited by Hans-Dieter Mutschler, 219–47. Freiburg im
Breisgau: Herder, 2001.

———. "Christology within an Evolutionary View of the World."
In *Theological Investigations* 5:157–92, translated by Karl-H.
Kruger. Baltimore: Helicon, 1966.

———. "The Concept of Mystery in Catholic Theology." In
Theological Investigations 4:36–73, translated by Kevin
Smyth. New York: Crossroad, 1966.

———. "Current Problems in Christology." In *Theological
Investigations* 1:149–200, translated by Cornelius Ernst. 2nd
ed. Baltimore: Helicon, 1965.

———. "The Doctrine of the 'Spiritual Senses' in the Middle
Ages." In *Theological Investigations* 16:104–34, translated by
David Morland. New York: Seabury, 1979.

———. *The Dynamic Element in the Church*. Translated by W. J.
O'Hara. Quaestiones Disputatae 12. New York: Herder and
Herder, 1964.

———. *Encounters with Silence*. Westminster, MD: Newman Press, 1960.

———. *Everyday Faith*. New York: Herder and Herder, 1968.

———. "The Exercises Today." In *Christian at the Crossroads*, translated by V. Green, 70–74. New York: Seabury, 1975.

———. *Foundations of Christian Faith: An Introduction to the Idea of Christianity*. New York: Seabury, 1978.

———. *Geist in Welt: Zur Metaphysik der endlichen Erkenntnis bei Thomas von Aquin*. 3rd ed. München: Kösel, 1957.

———. *Glaube, der die Erde Liebt: Christliche Besinnung im Alltag der Welt*. 3rd ed. Freiburg: Herder, 1967.

———. *Grace in Freedom*. New York: Herder and Herder, 1969.

———. *Hearers of the Word*. Edited by Johannes Baptist Metz. Translated by Michael Richards. New York: Herder and Herder, 1969.

———. "The Hiddenness of God." In *Theological Investigations* 16:227–43, translated by David Morland. New York: Crossroad, 1979.

———. *Hörer des Wortes: Zur Grundlegung einer Religionsphilosophie*. Edited by Johannes Baptist Metz. München: Kösel, 1963.

———. "Ignatius of Loyola Speaks to a Modern Jesuit." In *Ignatius of Loyola*, edited by Paul Imhof, 9–38. London: Collins, 1979.

———. "An Investigation of the Incomprehensibility of God in St Thomas Aquinas." In *Theological Investigations* 16:244–54, translated by David Morland. New York: Crossroad, 1979.

———. *Karl Rahner im Gespräch*. Edited by Paul Imhof and Hubert Biallowons. München: Kösel, 1982.

———. *Karl Rahner in Dialogue: Conversations and Interviews, 1965–1982*. Edited by Paul Imhof and Hubert Biallowons. Translated by Harvey D. Egan. New York: Crossroad, 1986.

————. "Mystical Experience and Mystical Theology." In *Theological Investigations* 17:90–99, translated by Margaret Kohl. New York: Crossroad, 1981.

————. "On Martin Heidegger." In *Karl Rahner: The Philosophical Foundations*, by Thomas Sheehan, xi–xii. Athens, OH: Ohio University Press, 1987.

————. "On the Theology of the Incarnation." In *Theological Investigations* 4:103–120, translated by Kevin Smyth. Baltimore: Helicon, 1966.

————. "Oneness and Threefoldness of God in Discussion with Islam." In *Theological Investigations* 18:105–21, translated by Edward Quinn. New York: Crossroad, 1983.

————. "Reconciliation and Vicarious Representation." In *Theological Investigations* 21:255–69, translated by Hugh M. Riley. London: Darton, Longman & Todd, 1988.

————. "Reflections on the Unity of the Love of Neighbour and the Love of God." In *Theological Investigations* 6:231–49, translated by Karl-H. Kruger and Boniface Kruger. London: Darton, Longman & Todd, 1969.

————. "Religious Enthusiasm and the Experience of Grace." In *Theological Investigations* 16:35–51, translated by David Morland. New York: Seabury, 1979.

————. *Sämtliche Werke*. Vol. 4, *Hörer des Wortes*, edited by Albert Raffelt. Solothurn, Düsseldorf: Benziger, 1997.

————. "Some Implications of the Scholastic Concept of Uncreated Grace." In *Theological Investigations* 1:319–46, translated by Cornelius Ernst. Baltimore: Helicon, 1969.

————. "Some Theses on Prayer." In *Theological Investigations*, translated by Karl-H. Kruger, 5:419–38. Baltimore: Helicon, 1966.

————. *Spirit in the World*. Translated by William Dych. New York: Herder and Herder, 1968.

————. "Theos in the New Testament." In *Theological*

Investigations 1:79–148, translated by Cornelius Ernst. Baltimore: Helicon, 1961.

———. "Thomas Aquinas." In *Everyday Faith*, 185–90. New York: Herder and Herder, 1968.

———. "Thomas Aquinas on Truth." In *Theological Investigations* 13:13–31, translated by David Bourke. New York: Seabury, 1975.

———. *The Trinity*. Translated by Joseph Donceel. New York: Crossroad, 1997.

———. "The Two Basic Types of Christology." In *Theological Investigations* 13:213–23, translated by David Bourke. New York: Seabury, 1975.

———. *Verantwortung der Theologie im Dialog mit Naturwissenschaften und Gesellschaftstheorie*. Freiburg im Breisgau: Herder, 2001.

———. *Vor dem Geheimnis Gottes den Menschen verstehen: Karl Rahner zum 80. Geburtstag*. München: Schnell & Steiner, 1984.

———. *Worte ins Schweigen*. Innsbruck, Leipzip: Rauch, 1938.

Rahner, Karl, ed. *Encyclopedia of Theology: The Concise Sacramentum Mundi*. New York: Seabury, 1975.

Rahner, Karl, and Meinold Krauss. *I Remember: An Autobiographical Interview with Meinold Krauss*. New York: Crossroad, 1985.

Rankin, W. Duncan. "Carnal Union with Christ in the Theology of T. F. Torrance." PhD diss., University of Edinburgh, 1997.

Rauser, Randal. "Rahner's Rule: An Emperor without Clothes?" *International Journal of Systematic Theology* 7, no. 1 (January 1, 2005): 81–94.

"Religious Studies at Stanford—Faculty." Accessed May 2, 2011. http://www.stanford.edu/dept/relstud/faculty.html.

Reymond, Robert L. *A New Systematic Theology of the Christian Faith*. Nashville: T. Nelson, 1998.

Ridderbos, Herman N. *Paul: An Outline of His Theology.* Grand Rapids: Eerdmans, 1977.

Rousselot, Pierre. *The Eyes of Faith: Answer to Two Attacks.* New York: Fordham University Press, 1990.

———. *The Intellectualism of Saint Thomas.* Translated by James E. O'Mahony. London: Sheed & Ward, 1935.

Scheeben, Matthias Joseph. *A Manual of Catholic Theology: Based on Scheeben's "Dogmatik."* London: Kegan Paul, Trench, Trübner, 1901.

———. *The Mysteries of Christianity.* St. Louis: B. Herder Book Co., 1947.

———. *Nature and Grace.* Eugene, OR: Wipf & Stock, 2009.

Sheehan, Thomas. *Karl Rahner: The Philosophical Foundations.* Athens, OH: Ohio University Press, 1987.

———. "Pierre Rousselot and the Dynamism of Human Spirit." *Gregorianum* 66, no. 2 (1985): 241–67.

Strimple, Robert B. *Modern Roman Catholic Theology.* Philadelphia: Westminster Theological Seminary, 1994.

Stump, Eleonore. *Aquinas.* London, New York: Routledge, 2003.

Sutton, M. L. "*Mysterium Christi*: The Christologies of Maurice de La Taille and Karl Rahner." *International Journal of Systematic Theology* 10, no. 4 (2008): 416–30.

"Thesaurus Linguae Graecae." Accessed November 15, 2011. http://stephanus.tlg.uci.edu/inst/textsearch.

Thomas Aquinas. *Compendium of Theology.* Oxford: Oxford University Press, 2009.

———. *Summa contra Gentiles.* Translated by Charles J. O'Neil. Garden City, NY: Hanover House, 1957.

———. *Summa Theologiae: Latin Text and English Translation, Introductions, Notes, Appendices, and Glossaries.* Cambridge: Blackfriars/New York: McGraw-Hill, 1964.

———. *Summa Theologiae: Questions on God.* Edited by

Brian Davies and Brian Leftow. Cambridge/New York: Cambridge University Press, 2006.

———. "Summa Theologica." *Christian Classics Ethereal Library.* Accessed May 10, 2011. http://www.ccel.org/ccel/aquinas /summa.txt.

Thompson, John. *Modern Trinitarian Perspectives.* Oxford/New York: Oxford University Press, 1994.

Tipton, Lane G. "The Function of Perichoresis and the Divine Incomprehensibility." *Westminster Theological Journal* 64 (2002): 289–306.

———. "The Triune Personal God: Trinitarian Theology in the Thought of Cornelius Van Til." PhD diss., Westminster Theological Seminary, 2004.

———. "Union with Christ: Its Foundational Status and Fundamental Structure (Part 1)." Class lecture presented at Westminster Theological Seminary, Glenside, PA, March 12, 2010.

Turretin, Francis. *Institutes of Elenctic Theology.* Translated by James T. Dennison. 3 vols. Phillipsburg, NJ: P&R Publishing, 1997.

Van Genderen, J., and W. H. Velema. *Concise Reformed Dogmatics.* Translated by Gerrit Bilkes and Ed M. van der Maas. Phillipsburg, NJ: P&R Publishing, 2008.

Van Til, Cornelius. *The Confession of 1967: Its Theological Background and Ecumenical Significance.* Philadelphia: Presbyterian and Reformed, 1967.

———. *An Introduction to Systematic Theology.* Phillipsburg, NJ: Presbyterian and Reformed, 1974.

———. *Introduction to Systematic Theology: Prolegomena and the Doctrines of Revelation, Scripture, and God.* 2nd ed. Phillipsburg, NJ: P&R Publishing, 2007.

———. *A Survey of Christian Epistemology.* 2nd ed. Phillipsburg, NJ: Presbyterian and Reformed, 1980.

Viller, Marcel, and Karl Rahner. *Aszese und Mystik in der Väterzeit: Ein Abriß.* Freiburg im Breisgau: Herder, 1939.

Visser, Sandra, and Thomas Williams. *Anselm.* Great Medieval Thinkers. Oxford, New York: Oxford University Press, 2009.

Vorgrimler, Herbert. "Karl Rahner: The Theologian's Contribution." In *Vatican II by Those Who Were There*, edited by Alberic Stacpoole, 32–46. London: G. Chapman, 1986.

———. *Understanding Karl Rahner: An Introduction to His Life and Thought.* New York: Crossroad, 1986.

Vos, Geerhardus. *Biblical Theology: Old and New Testaments.* Edinburgh, Carlisle, PA: Banner of Truth, 1975.

———. *The Eschatology of the Old Testament.* Phillipsburg, NJ: P&R Publishing, 2001.

———. *The Pauline Eschatology.* Phillipsburg, NJ: P&R Publishing, 1994.

———. *Redemptive History and Biblical Interpretation: The Shorter Writings of Geerhardus Vos.* Edited by Richard B. Gaffin, Jr. Phillipsburg, NJ: P&R Publishing, 2001.

Wawrykow, Joseph. "Hypostatic Union." In *The Theology of Thomas Aquinas*, edited by Rik van Nieuwenhove and Joseph Wawrykow, 222–51. Notre Dame, IN: University of Notre Dame Press, 2005.

Willis-Watkins, David. "The *Unio Mystica* and the Assurance of Faith according to Calvin." In *Calvin: Erbe und Auftrag: Festschrift für Wilhelm Heinrich Neuser zum 65. Geburtstag*, edited by Willem van't Spijker, 77–84. Kampen: Kok, 1991.

Wisser, Richard, ed. *Martin Heidegger im Gespräch.* Freiburg im Breisgau, München: K. Alber, 1970.

INDEX OF SCRIPTURE

INDEX OF SUBJECTS
AND NAMES